Table of Contents

Chapter 1: Introduction to Cyber Warfare Strategy 4
- Understanding Cyber Warfare 4
- Importance of Cyber Warfare Strategy 5
- Overview of Cyber Warfare Tactics 6

Chapter 2: Planning for Cyber Warfare 8
- Assessing Vulnerabilities 8
- Developing a Cyber Warfare Strategy 10
- Implementing Cyber Security Measures 11

Chapter 3: Cyber Warfare in the Healthcare Industry 12
- Risks and Threats in Healthcare 13
- Securing Patient Data 14
- Protecting Medical Devices from Cyber Attacks 16

Chapter 4: Cyber Warfare in the Financial Sector 17
- Financial Cyber Threats 17
- Securing Financial Transactions 18
- Protecting Customer Information 20

Chapter 5: Cyber Warfare in the Government Sector 22
- Government Cyber Security Challenges 22
- Securing Government Networks 23
- Protecting Critical Infrastructure 25

Chapter 6: Cyber Warfare in the Energy Sector 26
- Cyber Threats to Energy Infrastructure 26
- Securing Energy Grids 28
- Protecting Oil and Gas Operations 30

Chapter 7: Cyber Warfare in the Education Sector 31
- Cyber Security in Schools and Universities 31
- Securing Student Data 32
- Protecting Educational Resources 34

Chapter 8: Cyber Warfare for Small Businesses 35

Small Business Cyber Security Risks 35
Implementing Cost-Effective Cyber Security Measures 37
Protecting Customer Information 38

Chapter 9: Cyber Warfare for Non-Profit Organizations 39
Cyber Security Challenges for Non-Profits 39
Securing Donor Information 41
Protecting Organizational Data 42

Chapter 10: Cyber Warfare in the Transportation Industry 44
Cyber Threats to Transportation Systems 44
Securing Transportation Networks 45
Protecting Passenger Information 47

Chapter 11: Cyber Warfare in the Telecommunications Sector 48
Telecommunications Cyber Security Risks 48
Securing Communication Networks 50
Protecting Customer Privacy 51

Chapter 12: Cyber Warfare in the Defense Industry 52
Military Cyber Threats 52
Securing Defense Networks 53
Protecting Classified Information 55

Chapter 13: Conclusion and Future Trends in Cyber Warfare Strategy 56
Recap of Cyber Warfare Strategy 57
Emerging Trends in Cyber Security 58
Recommendations for Professionals in Cyber Warfare 59

Case Studies of Notable Cyber Warfare Incidents 62
Stuxnet: 62
SolarWinds Attack: 66
NotPetya: 70
The Sony Pictures Hack: 74
The Office of Personnel Management (OPM) Data Breach: 78

Frameworks and Standards 82
NIST Cybersecurity Framework: A Comprehensive Summary 82

- ISO/IEC 27001: A Comprehensive Summary 87
- MITRE ATT&CK Framework: A Comprehensive Summary 92
- CIS Controls: A Comprehensive Summary 97

Tools and Technologies 102
- SIEM Solutions (Security Information and Event Management): A Comprehensive Summary 102
- Endpoint Detection and Response (EDR): A Comprehensive Summary 107
- Intrusion Detection Systems (IDS) / Intrusion Prevention Systems (IPS): A Comprehensive Summary 112

Best Practices 116
- Incident Response Planning 116
  - Incident Response Planning: A Comprehensive Summary 116
- Threat Intelligence 121
  - Threat Intelligence: A Comprehensive Summary 121
- Employee Training and Awareness: A Comprehensive Summary 125

Emerging Trends 130
- Artificial Intelligence in Cybersecurity 130
- Zero Trust Architecture: A Comprehensive Summary 135
- Cyber Resilience 140

Additional Reading and Resources 145
Professional Organizations and Certifications 146

Chapter 1: Introduction to Cyber Warfare Strategy

Understanding Cyber Warfare

Cyber warfare is a growing concern in today's digital age, with attacks becoming more sophisticated and damaging than ever before. Professionals across various industries must be prepared to combat these threats effectively. In this subchapter, we will delve into the intricacies of cyber warfare and provide strategies for planning and mitigating potential attacks in different sectors.

One key aspect of understanding cyber warfare is recognizing the various tactics and techniques used by malicious actors. From phishing scams and ransomware attacks to DDoS (Distributed Denial of Service) assaults, cybercriminals have a range of tools at their disposal to infiltrate systems and steal sensitive information. Professionals must stay abreast of these evolving threats to effectively defend against them.

When planning for cyber warfare in the healthcare industry, professionals must prioritize the security of patient data and critical systems. With the increasing digitization of medical records and the reliance on interconnected devices, healthcare organizations are prime targets for cyber attacks. Implementing robust cybersecurity measures, conducting regular audits, and training staff on best practices are essential steps in fortifying defenses against potential threats.

In the financial sector, cyber warfare poses a significant risk to banks, investment firms, and other financial institutions. With the potential for financial loss and reputational damage, professionals must prioritize cybersecurity as a top priority. Implementing multi-factor authentication, encryption protocols, and continuous monitoring of networks are critical steps in safeguarding sensitive financial data from cyber attacks.

In the government sector, the stakes are even higher, as cyber attacks can have far-reaching implications on national security and public safety. Professionals in this sector must collaborate with intelligence agencies, law enforcement, and cybersecurity experts to develop robust defense strategies. Implementing secure communication channels, conducting regular threat assessments, and investing in cybersecurity training for government employees are crucial steps in protecting critical infrastructure from cyber threats.

Importance of Cyber Warfare Strategy

In today's digital age, the importance of having a solid cyber warfare strategy cannot be overstated. Cyber warfare refers to the use of technology to disrupt or sabotage the information systems of a target, whether it be a government, organization, or individual. With the increasing reliance on technology in various sectors, the need for a comprehensive cyber warfare strategy is more crucial than ever.

One of the key reasons why having a cyber warfare strategy is essential is to protect sensitive information. In sectors such as healthcare, financial services, and government, the data stored on their systems is highly confidential and valuable. A cyber attack can not only result in financial losses but also compromise the privacy and security of individuals. By having a well-thought-out cyber warfare strategy in place, organizations can safeguard their data and prevent unauthorized access.

Moreover, a cyber warfare strategy is necessary to maintain operational continuity. In industries like energy, transportation, and telecommunications, any disruption in their information systems can have far-reaching consequences. A cyber attack can lead to service outages, delays, and even safety hazards. By having a proactive cyber warfare strategy, organizations can minimize the impact of attacks and ensure their operations remain uninterrupted.

Additionally, having a cyber warfare strategy is crucial for compliance with regulations and standards. In sectors like healthcare, education, and defense, there are strict regulations in place to protect sensitive information and ensure data security. Failure to comply with these regulations can result in hefty fines and damage to the organization's reputation. A robust cyber warfare strategy can help organizations meet these requirements and demonstrate their commitment to cybersecurity.

Overall, having a cyber warfare strategy is vital for organizations of all sizes and industries. Whether it is planning for cyber warfare in the healthcare industry, financial sector, government sector, or any other sector, having a proactive approach to cybersecurity is essential. By investing in the right tools, technologies, and training, organizations can effectively defend against cyber threats and safeguard their operations and reputation.

Overview of Cyber Warfare Tactics

In the world of cyber warfare, tactics play a critical role in determining the success or failure of an attack. Understanding the various tactics employed by cyber attackers is essential for professionals in any industry to effectively plan for and defend against potential threats. This subchapter will provide an overview of some common cyber warfare tactics that professionals should be aware of in order to protect their organizations and assets.

One of the most common cyber warfare tactics is phishing, where attackers use deceptive emails or messages to trick individuals into revealing sensitive information such as passwords or financial data. Phishing attacks can be highly effective, as they often rely on social engineering techniques to manipulate victims into taking actions that compromise their security. Professionals should educate themselves and their employees on how to recognize and avoid phishing attempts in order to mitigate the risk of falling victim to such attacks.

Another tactic used in cyber warfare is malware, which refers to malicious software designed to infiltrate and damage computer systems. Malware can take many forms, including viruses, worms, and ransomware, and can be distributed through various means such as infected email attachments or compromised websites. Professionals should implement robust cybersecurity measures, such as firewalls and antivirus software, to protect their networks from malware attacks and regularly update their systems to patch vulnerabilities that could be exploited by cyber attackers.

Denial of service (DoS) attacks are another common tactic used in cyber warfare, where attackers overwhelm a target system with an excessive amount of traffic in order to disrupt its normal operation. These attacks can result in significant downtime and financial losses for organizations, making it crucial for professionals to have contingency plans in place to mitigate the impact of DoS attacks. Implementing network monitoring tools and collaborating with internet service providers can help detect and mitigate DoS attacks before they cause serious damage.

In addition to these tactics, professionals should also be aware of the importance of encryption in protecting sensitive data from cyber threats. Encryption involves encoding information in such a way that only authorized parties can access it, making it an essential component of any cybersecurity strategy. By encrypting data both at rest and in transit, professionals can significantly reduce the risk of data breaches and unauthorized access, safeguarding their organization's most valuable assets from cyber attackers. Overall, understanding and implementing effective cyber warfare tactics is essential for professionals in any industry to secure their digital infrastructure and protect against the ever-evolving landscape of cyber threats.

Chapter 2: Planning for Cyber Warfare

Assessing Vulnerabilities

Assessing vulnerabilities is a critical step in planning for cyber warfare across various sectors. Understanding where weaknesses lie within an organization's systems and infrastructure is essential for developing effective defense strategies. By identifying vulnerabilities, professionals can prioritize their efforts to strengthen security measures and mitigate potential risks.

In the healthcare industry, assessing vulnerabilities is crucial due to the sensitive nature of patient data and the potential impact of cyber attacks on medical devices. Healthcare professionals must conduct thorough assessments to identify weak points in their systems, such as outdated software or inadequate encryption protocols. By addressing these vulnerabilities, healthcare organizations can better protect patient information and ensure the continued delivery of quality care.

Similarly, in the financial sector, assessing vulnerabilities is essential for safeguarding sensitive financial data and maintaining customer trust. Financial professionals must regularly evaluate their systems for weaknesses that could be exploited by cyber criminals. By conducting thorough assessments and implementing robust security measures, financial institutions can minimize the risk of data breaches and financial fraud.

In the government sector, assessing vulnerabilities is critical for protecting national security interests and ensuring the continuity of essential government services. Government professionals must identify potential weaknesses in their systems, such as outdated infrastructure or inadequate training for employees. By addressing these vulnerabilities, government agencies can better defend against cyber threats and safeguard sensitive information.

In the energy sector, assessing vulnerabilities is vital for protecting critical infrastructure and preventing disruptions to essential services. Energy professionals must evaluate their systems for weaknesses that could be exploited by cyber attackers, such as vulnerabilities in control systems or inadequate disaster recovery plans. By identifying and addressing these vulnerabilities, energy companies can enhance their resilience to cyber threats and maintain the reliability of their operations.

Developing a Cyber Warfare Strategy

In today's interconnected world, the threat of cyber warfare is a looming concern for professionals across various industries. Developing a robust cyber warfare strategy is crucial for organizations to protect their assets, data, and reputation from malicious cyber attacks. This subchapter will delve into the key considerations and steps that professionals should take to plan for cyber warfare effectively.

When planning for cyber warfare, professionals must first conduct a thorough risk assessment to identify potential vulnerabilities and threats. This assessment should involve evaluating the organization's systems, networks, and data to determine where potential weaknesses lie. By understanding the specific risks facing their organization, professionals can tailor their cyber warfare strategy to address these vulnerabilities effectively.

In the healthcare industry, the stakes are especially high when it comes to cyber warfare. Patient data and medical records are valuable targets for cyber attackers, making it essential for healthcare professionals to prioritize cybersecurity. Developing a cyber warfare strategy in the healthcare industry should involve implementing robust encryption measures, regularly updating software systems, and training staff on best practices for data security.

Similarly, professionals in the financial sector must be vigilant in planning for cyber warfare. Financial institutions are prime targets for cyber attacks due to the sensitive nature of the data they hold. Developing a cyber warfare strategy in the financial sector should focus on implementing multi-factor authentication, monitoring for suspicious activity, and collaborating with other institutions to share threat intelligence.

In the government sector, cyber warfare poses a significant threat to national security and public safety. Professionals in this sector must work closely with law enforcement agencies and cybersecurity experts to develop a comprehensive cyber warfare strategy. This strategy should include measures such as regular penetration testing, incident response planning, and information sharing with other government agencies. By taking a proactive approach to cyber warfare planning, professionals in the government sector can better protect critical infrastructure and national interests.

Implementing Cyber Security Measures

Implementing cyber security measures is crucial in today's digital age, where cyber attacks are becoming increasingly prevalent and sophisticated. As professionals in various sectors, it is imperative to plan and prepare for potential cyber warfare scenarios to protect sensitive data and infrastructure. By implementing robust cyber security measures, organizations can mitigate the risk of cyber threats and safeguard their operations.

In the healthcare industry, implementing cyber security measures is vital to protect patient data and ensure the continuity of medical services. Healthcare organizations must invest in advanced security technologies and protocols to safeguard electronic health records and medical devices from cyber attacks. By conducting regular risk assessments and training staff on cyber security best practices, healthcare professionals can enhance their resilience against cyber threats.

Similarly, in the financial sector, implementing cyber security measures is essential to protect financial transactions and customer information. Financial institutions must implement multi-layered security measures, such as encryption and access controls, to prevent unauthorized access to sensitive data. By monitoring network activity and conducting regular security audits, financial professionals can detect and respond to cyber threats in a timely manner.

In the government sector, implementing cyber security measures is critical to protect national security and public services. Government agencies must collaborate with cybersecurity experts and law enforcement agencies to develop comprehensive cyber security strategies. By implementing secure communication channels and implementing incident response plans, government professionals can effectively mitigate the impact of cyber attacks on critical infrastructure.

In the energy sector, implementing cyber security measures is essential to protect power grids and energy resources from cyber threats. Energy companies must invest in secure technologies and conduct regular security assessments to identify vulnerabilities in their systems. By implementing robust access controls and monitoring systems, energy professionals can prevent malicious actors from disrupting essential services and causing widespread damage.

Chapter 3: Cyber Warfare in the Healthcare Industry

Risks and Threats in Healthcare

In the realm of healthcare, the risks and threats posed by cyber warfare are particularly concerning. The sensitive nature of patient data and the critical role that healthcare institutions play in society make them attractive targets for malicious cyber actors. One of the primary risks in this sector is the potential for data breaches, where personal and medical information of patients could be compromised. This not only puts individuals at risk of identity theft and fraud but also jeopardizes the trust between patients and healthcare providers.

Another significant threat in the healthcare industry is the possibility of ransomware attacks. These attacks involve encrypting a healthcare organization's data and demanding a ransom for its release. In addition to the financial implications of paying a ransom, such attacks can disrupt healthcare services, putting patients' lives at risk. Moreover, the interconnected nature of healthcare systems means that an attack on one institution could have broader implications for the entire sector.

Furthermore, the increasing reliance on connected medical devices and telemedicine services has opened up new vulnerabilities in the healthcare industry. Hackers could potentially gain access to these devices and manipulate them to cause harm to patients. Similarly, the use of electronic health records and other digital systems in healthcare makes them susceptible to cyber attacks, which could result in the loss or alteration of critical patient information.

To mitigate these risks and threats, healthcare professionals must prioritize cybersecurity measures. This includes implementing robust security protocols, regularly updating software and systems, and providing staff with training on how to identify and respond to potential cyber threats. Additionally, healthcare organizations should collaborate with cybersecurity experts and government agencies to stay informed about emerging threats and best practices for cyber defense.

In conclusion, the risks and threats posed by cyber warfare in the healthcare industry are significant and must be taken seriously. By taking proactive steps to enhance cybersecurity measures, healthcare professionals can better protect patient data, ensure the continuity of healthcare services, and safeguard the integrity of the sector as a whole. It is essential for healthcare organizations to stay vigilant and prepared to respond effectively to cyber threats in order to uphold their duty of care to patients and maintain the trust of the public.

Securing Patient Data

In today's digital age, securing patient data is a critical aspect of any organization operating in the healthcare industry. The sensitive information contained in patient records, such as medical history, treatments, and personal details, must be protected from cyber threats to ensure patient confidentiality and trust. This subchapter will explore the importance of securing patient data and provide strategies for professionals in the healthcare sector to safeguard this information from cyber attacks.

One of the key challenges in securing patient data is the evolving nature of cyber threats. Hackers are constantly developing new techniques to breach security systems and access sensitive information. To combat these threats, professionals in the healthcare industry must stay informed about the latest cybersecurity trends and implement robust security measures to protect patient data. This may include encryption, multi-factor authentication, and regular security audits to identify and address vulnerabilities.

Another important aspect of securing patient data is compliance with regulations such as the Health Insurance Portability and Accountability Act (HIPAA) in the United States. HIPAA sets strict guidelines for the protection of patient information and imposes penalties for non-compliance. Professionals in the healthcare sector must ensure that their data security practices align with HIPAA requirements to avoid legal repercussions and maintain patient trust.

In addition to regulatory compliance, professionals in the healthcare industry must also consider the potential impact of a data breach on their organization's reputation and financial stability. A significant breach of patient data can result in costly lawsuits, damage to the organization's brand, and loss of patient trust. By implementing strong security measures and regularly assessing and updating their cybersecurity protocols, professionals can mitigate these risks and protect their organization from the devastating consequences of a data breach.

Overall, securing patient data is a complex and ongoing process that requires vigilance, expertise, and a commitment to protecting patient privacy. By staying informed about the latest cybersecurity threats, complying with regulations such as HIPAA, and implementing robust security measures, professionals in the healthcare industry can safeguard patient data and uphold the trust and confidentiality of their patients.

Protecting Medical Devices from Cyber Attacks

With the increasing reliance on medical devices in the healthcare industry, protecting these devices from cyber attacks has become a critical concern. Cyber attacks on medical devices can have serious consequences, including compromising patient safety and data security. In this subchapter, we will discuss strategies for protecting medical devices from cyber attacks.

One of the first steps in protecting medical devices from cyber attacks is to ensure that the devices are secure by design. This means that security features should be integrated into the devices from the initial design phase. Manufacturers should consider factors such as authentication, encryption, and secure communication protocols when developing medical devices to prevent vulnerabilities that could be exploited by cyber attackers.

In addition to secure design, it is important to regularly update and patch medical devices to address any known security vulnerabilities. Manufacturers should establish processes for monitoring and responding to security threats in a timely manner. Healthcare organizations should also implement security protocols for managing and updating medical devices to ensure that they remain protected against cyber attacks.

Furthermore, healthcare organizations should implement network segmentation to isolate medical devices from other systems and reduce the risk of lateral movement by cyber attackers. By segmenting networks, organizations can limit the potential impact of a cyber attack on medical devices and prevent unauthorized access to sensitive data.

Lastly, healthcare organizations should train staff on best practices for using and securing medical devices. Employees should be educated on the risks of cyber attacks and trained on how to detect and report suspicious activity. By creating a culture of cybersecurity awareness, healthcare organizations can help prevent cyber attacks on medical devices and protect patient safety and data security.

Chapter 4: Cyber Warfare in the Financial Sector

Financial Cyber Threats

Financial cyber threats pose a significant risk to businesses and organizations in the financial sector. These threats can come in the form of data breaches, ransomware attacks, phishing scams, and more. It is important for professionals in the financial sector to be aware of these threats and to have a comprehensive plan in place to prevent and respond to cyber attacks.

One of the key financial cyber threats that professionals need to be aware of is data breaches. Data breaches can result in the theft of sensitive financial information, such as customer account numbers and personal information. This can lead to financial loss for both the organization and its customers, as well as damage to the organization's reputation. To prevent data breaches, professionals in the financial sector should implement strong data security measures, such as encryption and multi-factor authentication.

Another common financial cyber threat is ransomware attacks. Ransomware is a type of malware that encrypts a victim's files and demands payment in exchange for the decryption key. These attacks can be devastating for financial organizations, as they can result in the loss of critical data and disrupt operations. To protect against ransomware attacks, professionals should regularly back up their data, keep their software up to date, and educate employees about the dangers of phishing emails.

Phishing scams are another prevalent financial cyber threat that professionals need to be vigilant about. Phishing scams involve sending fraudulent emails or messages that appear to be from a reputable source, such as a bank or financial institution. These emails often contain links or attachments that, when clicked on, can lead to malware infections or the theft of sensitive information. To protect against phishing scams, professionals should train employees to recognize and report suspicious emails, and implement email filtering and anti-phishing software.

In conclusion, financial cyber threats are a serious concern for professionals in the financial sector. By understanding the various types of threats, implementing strong security measures, and educating employees about cyber risks, professionals can better protect their organizations from cyber attacks. It is essential for professionals in the financial sector to have a comprehensive plan in place to prevent and respond to cyber threats, in order to safeguard their organization's financial assets and reputation.

Securing Financial Transactions

In today's digital age, securing financial transactions has become more critical than ever before. As technology continues to advance, so do the tactics used by cyber criminals to exploit vulnerabilities in financial systems. For professionals in various industries, understanding the importance of securing financial transactions is paramount to protecting sensitive data and preventing costly breaches.

In the healthcare industry, securing financial transactions is crucial to safeguarding patient information and maintaining trust in the integrity of healthcare systems. With the rise of electronic health records and online payment systems, healthcare professionals must implement robust cybersecurity measures to prevent unauthorized access to sensitive financial data.

Similarly, in the financial sector, protecting financial transactions is essential to safeguarding the assets of individuals and organizations. With the increasing prevalence of online banking and mobile payment platforms, financial institutions must continually assess and strengthen their cybersecurity defenses to prevent data breaches and financial fraud.

In the government sector, securing financial transactions is vital to protecting taxpayer funds and ensuring the efficient operation of government agencies. As government services increasingly move online, government professionals must prioritize cybersecurity measures to prevent cyber attacks that could disrupt financial transactions and compromise sensitive government data.

In the energy sector, securing financial transactions is critical to maintaining the stability of the global energy supply chain. With the increasing interconnectedness of energy networks and the rise of smart grid technologies, energy professionals must implement robust cybersecurity measures to prevent cyber attacks that could disrupt financial transactions and threaten the reliability of energy systems. By prioritizing cybersecurity and implementing best practices for securing financial transactions, professionals in various industries can protect sensitive data, prevent costly breaches, and safeguard the integrity of financial systems in an increasingly digital world.

Protecting Customer Information

Protecting customer information is a crucial aspect of any organization's cybersecurity strategy. In today's digital age, where data breaches and cyber attacks are becoming increasingly common, it is essential for professionals in various industries to take proactive measures to safeguard their customers' sensitive information. This subchapter will discuss the importance of protecting customer information and provide practical tips on how to do so effectively.

One of the first steps in protecting customer information is to implement strong encryption protocols. Encryption helps to secure data by converting it into a code that can only be deciphered with the correct decryption key. By encrypting customer data both in transit and at rest, organizations can significantly reduce the risk of unauthorized access and data theft. Professionals in industries such as healthcare, finance, and government must ensure that they are using the latest encryption technologies to protect sensitive customer information.

Another important aspect of protecting customer information is to establish robust access controls. By limiting access to sensitive data to only authorized personnel, organizations can minimize the risk of insider threats and unauthorized access. Access controls should include strong password policies, multi-factor authentication, and regular access audits to ensure that only those who need to access customer information are able to do so. Professionals in sectors such as energy, education, and transportation must prioritize access control measures to protect customer data from potential cyber threats.

In addition to encryption and access controls, professionals should also implement regular security training and awareness programs for employees. Human error is often a leading cause of data breaches, so educating staff on best practices for handling customer information can help to mitigate the risk of accidental data exposure. Training programs should cover topics such as phishing awareness, social engineering tactics, and proper data handling procedures. By empowering employees to be vigilant and proactive in protecting customer information, organizations can strengthen their overall cybersecurity posture.

Furthermore, professionals should regularly conduct vulnerability assessments and penetration testing to identify and address potential security weaknesses in their systems. By proactively testing for vulnerabilities and addressing them before they can be exploited by malicious actors, organizations can reduce the likelihood of a data breach. Vulnerability assessments should be conducted on a regular basis, and any identified vulnerabilities should be promptly remediated to protect customer information. Professionals in industries such as telecommunications, defense, and small businesses must prioritize vulnerability management to defend against cyber threats effectively.

In conclusion, protecting customer information is a critical component of any organization's cybersecurity strategy. By implementing strong encryption protocols, access controls, security training programs, and vulnerability assessments, professionals can safeguard customer data from potential cyber threats. In today's digital landscape, where data breaches are on the rise, it is essential for professionals in various industries to prioritize the protection of customer information to maintain trust and credibility with their clients.

Chapter 5: Cyber Warfare in the Government Sector

Government Cyber Security Challenges

Government cyber security challenges are among the most critical issues facing nations in the modern digital age. With the increasing sophistication of cyber threats, governments around the world are struggling to protect their sensitive data and infrastructure from malicious actors. From state-sponsored attacks to cyber espionage, the challenges facing government entities are vast and complex.

One of the primary challenges facing government cyber security efforts is the sheer volume of attacks targeting government systems. With the rise of nation-state actors and cyber criminal organizations, governments are facing a constant barrage of attacks on their networks and systems. These attacks can range from simple phishing emails to complex malware designed to infiltrate government networks and steal sensitive information.

Another major challenge facing government cyber security is the issue of insider threats. While external threats are a significant concern, insiders with access to sensitive government data can pose a significant risk to national security. Whether through malicious intent or accidental actions, insider threats can result in the compromise of critical government systems and information.

Additionally, the interconnected nature of government systems presents a unique challenge for cyber security professionals. Government agencies often rely on shared networks and infrastructure, making it difficult to secure individual systems without impacting overall operations. This interconnectedness also means that a breach in one agency's systems can have far-reaching consequences for the entire government.

Lastly, the rapid pace of technological advancement presents a challenge for government cyber security efforts. As new technologies emerge, governments must adapt their cyber security strategies to address the evolving threat landscape. This requires a proactive approach to identifying and mitigating potential vulnerabilities in government systems, as well as ongoing investment in training and education for government cyber security professionals.

Securing Government Networks

Protecting government networks from cyber threats is a critical task that requires constant vigilance and strategic planning. Government agencies are prime targets for cyber attacks due to the sensitive nature of the information they store and the potential impact of a successful breach. As professionals working in the government sector, it is essential to understand the unique challenges and risks associated with securing government networks.

One of the key strategies for securing government networks is to implement robust cybersecurity measures that encompass both prevention and detection. This includes deploying firewalls, antivirus software, intrusion detection systems, and encryption technologies to safeguard sensitive data and prevent unauthorized access. Regular security audits and penetration testing can help identify vulnerabilities and weaknesses in the network infrastructure, allowing for timely remediation before they can be exploited by malicious actors.

In addition to technical safeguards, government agencies must also prioritize employee training and awareness programs to educate staff about the importance of cybersecurity best practices. Phishing attacks, social engineering tactics, and other forms of cyber threats often target unsuspecting employees who may inadvertently compromise network security. By promoting a culture of cybersecurity awareness and providing ongoing training, government agencies can empower their workforce to recognize and respond to potential threats effectively.

Collaboration and information sharing are crucial components of a successful cybersecurity strategy for government networks. By establishing partnerships with other government agencies, law enforcement organizations, and cybersecurity experts, government professionals can access valuable threat intelligence, resources, and expertise to enhance their defensive capabilities. Sharing information about emerging threats, attack patterns, and best practices can help government agencies stay ahead of cyber adversaries and proactively defend against evolving threats.

As cyber threats continue to evolve and grow in sophistication, government professionals must remain adaptable and proactive in their approach to securing government networks. By staying informed about the latest cybersecurity trends, technologies, and regulations, government agencies can strengthen their defenses and better protect critical assets and infrastructure from cyber attacks. By implementing a comprehensive cybersecurity strategy that combines technical controls, employee training, collaboration, and information sharing, government professionals can effectively mitigate risks and safeguard government networks against cyber threats.

Protecting Critical Infrastructure

Protecting critical infrastructure is a top priority in the realm of cyber warfare. As professionals in various sectors such as healthcare, finance, government, energy, education, small businesses, non-profit organizations, transportation, telecommunications, and defense, it is crucial to have a comprehensive strategy in place to safeguard against cyber attacks that could potentially disrupt operations and compromise sensitive information.

In the healthcare industry, protecting critical infrastructure means ensuring the security of patient records, medical devices, and communication systems. Hospitals and healthcare facilities must implement robust cybersecurity measures to prevent unauthorized access to patient data and minimize the risk of ransomware attacks that could disrupt patient care. It is essential for healthcare professionals to regularly update software, conduct security audits, and train staff on best practices for handling sensitive information.

Similarly, in the financial sector, protecting critical infrastructure involves safeguarding banking systems, payment processing networks, and customer data. Financial institutions must invest in advanced cybersecurity technologies to detect and respond to threats in real-time. Regular security assessments, penetration testing, and employee training are essential to mitigate risks and prevent financial fraud or data breaches that could have far-reaching consequences for the economy.

In the government sector, protecting critical infrastructure is essential to national security and public safety. Government agencies must collaborate with cybersecurity experts to identify vulnerabilities in critical systems and develop contingency plans to respond to cyber attacks. By implementing robust cybersecurity measures, government professionals can protect sensitive information, prevent data breaches, and maintain public trust in the integrity of government operations.

In the energy sector, protecting critical infrastructure involves securing power plants, pipelines, and distribution networks from cyber threats. Energy professionals must implement multi-layered security defenses to detect and mitigate cyber attacks that could disrupt the supply of electricity, oil, and natural gas. By investing in cybersecurity training, threat intelligence, and incident response capabilities, energy companies can enhance their resilience to cyber threats and ensure the reliability of critical infrastructure.

Chapter 6: Cyber Warfare in the Energy Sector

Cyber Threats to Energy Infrastructure

In recent years, cyber threats to energy infrastructure have become increasingly prevalent and sophisticated. The interconnected nature of the energy sector makes it a prime target for cyber attacks, as disruptions in one part of the infrastructure can have cascading effects throughout the entire system. This subchapter will explore the various cyber threats facing the energy sector and provide strategies for professionals to protect critical energy infrastructure from these threats.

One of the most common cyber threats to energy infrastructure is ransomware attacks. These attacks involve malicious actors gaining access to a system and encrypting data, demanding payment in exchange for restoring access. In the energy sector, ransomware attacks can disrupt operations, leading to power outages and other potentially catastrophic consequences. Professionals in the energy sector must be vigilant in implementing robust cybersecurity measures to prevent ransomware attacks and mitigate their impact if they occur.

Another significant cyber threat to energy infrastructure is advanced persistent threats (APTs). APTs are long-term, targeted attacks in which adversaries gain unauthorized access to a system and remain undetected for extended periods. These attacks can be particularly damaging in the energy sector, where adversaries may seek to disrupt critical infrastructure or steal sensitive information. Professionals in the energy sector must be proactive in monitoring for APTs and implementing defense mechanisms to detect and respond to these threats effectively.

Phishing attacks are also a common cyber threat to energy infrastructure. Phishing attacks involve sending fraudulent emails or messages to individuals within an organization, tricking them into revealing sensitive information or downloading malicious software. In the energy sector, phishing attacks can compromise critical systems and lead to data breaches or other security incidents. Professionals in the energy sector must educate employees about the risks of phishing attacks and implement robust email security measures to prevent these threats from succeeding.

In addition to external cyber threats, professionals in the energy sector must also be aware of insider threats. Insider threats involve individuals within an organization who misuse their access to systems or data for malicious purposes. In the energy sector, insider threats can be particularly damaging, as individuals with insider knowledge may be able to cause significant disruptions to critical infrastructure. Professionals in the energy sector must implement strict access controls and monitoring mechanisms to detect and prevent insider threats before they can cause harm.

Overall, cyber threats to energy infrastructure are a significant concern for professionals in the energy sector. By understanding the various threats facing the sector and implementing robust cybersecurity measures, professionals can protect critical energy infrastructure from cyber attacks and ensure the reliable and secure operation of energy systems.

Securing Energy Grids

The energy sector is a critical infrastructure that is increasingly becoming a target for cyber attacks. As our reliance on technology continues to grow, so does the vulnerability of our energy grids to malicious actors. Securing energy grids is essential to ensure the stability and reliability of our power supply. In this subchapter, we will discuss the importance of securing energy grids and provide strategies for professionals to protect against cyber threats.

One of the key challenges in securing energy grids is the interconnected nature of the grid. Energy grids are comprised of a complex network of power plants, transmission lines, and distribution systems that are all interconnected. This interconnectedness makes it difficult to isolate and protect individual components of the grid from cyber attacks. Professionals in the energy sector must develop a comprehensive security strategy that takes into account the entire energy grid and all of its components.

In order to secure energy grids, professionals must first identify potential vulnerabilities in the grid. This can be done through regular security assessments and penetration testing to identify weaknesses in the system. Once vulnerabilities are identified, professionals can then develop and implement security measures to protect against cyber threats. This may include implementing firewalls, intrusion detection systems, and encryption protocols to safeguard the grid from malicious actors.

Another important aspect of securing energy grids is establishing clear communication and coordination between different entities within the energy sector. This includes utility companies, government agencies, and regulatory bodies. By working together and sharing information, professionals can better respond to cyber threats and coordinate a unified response in the event of a cyber attack. Collaboration and information sharing are key components of any effective cyber security strategy for energy grids.

In conclusion, securing energy grids is a critical task that requires the cooperation and coordination of professionals across the energy sector. By identifying vulnerabilities, implementing security measures, and establishing clear communication channels, professionals can protect our energy grids from cyber threats and ensure the stability and reliability of our power supply. It is essential that professionals in the energy sector prioritize cyber security and take proactive steps to safeguard our energy infrastructure from malicious actors.

Protecting Oil and Gas Operations

Protecting oil and gas operations from cyber warfare is crucial in today's interconnected world. As the energy sector becomes increasingly digitized, the risk of cyber attacks on critical infrastructure continues to grow. In order to safeguard against these threats, professionals in the oil and gas industry must implement robust cybersecurity measures to protect their operations from potential attacks.

One of the key steps in protecting oil and gas operations from cyber warfare is to conduct regular risk assessments. By identifying potential vulnerabilities in their systems and networks, professionals can proactively address security gaps before they are exploited by malicious actors. This requires a thorough understanding of the various cyber threats facing the industry, as well as the potential impact of a successful attack on critical infrastructure.

In addition to risk assessments, professionals in the oil and gas industry must also implement strong access controls to prevent unauthorized individuals from gaining access to sensitive systems and data. This includes implementing multi-factor authentication, role-based access controls, and regular monitoring of user activity to detect any suspicious behavior. By limiting access to only those who need it, professionals can reduce the risk of insider threats and unauthorized access to critical infrastructure.

Furthermore, professionals in the oil and gas industry should also invest in robust incident response capabilities to quickly detect, respond to, and recover from cyber attacks. This includes developing detailed response plans, conducting regular training exercises, and establishing partnerships with law enforcement agencies and cybersecurity experts to ensure a coordinated response in the event of a cyber attack. By being prepared to quickly mitigate the impact of an attack, professionals can minimize downtime and protect their operations from costly disruptions.

Overall, protecting oil and gas operations from cyber warfare requires a proactive and comprehensive approach to cybersecurity. By conducting regular risk assessments, implementing strong access controls, and investing in incident response capabilities, professionals can safeguard their critical infrastructure from potential cyber threats. In today's digital age, it is essential for professionals in the oil and gas industry to prioritize cybersecurity and take steps to protect their operations from the growing threat of cyber attacks.

Chapter 7: Cyber Warfare in the Education Sector

Cyber Security in Schools and Universities

Cyber security in schools and universities is a crucial aspect of protecting sensitive information and ensuring the safety of students and staff. Educational institutions are increasingly becoming targets for cyber attacks, as they store a vast amount of personal data, research, and financial information. It is essential for professionals in the education sector to have a comprehensive cyber warfare strategy in place to mitigate the risks and prevent potential breaches.

One key aspect of cyber security in schools and universities is implementing robust data encryption protocols to safeguard sensitive information. This includes encrypting student records, financial data, and research findings to prevent unauthorized access and data theft. Additionally, regular security audits and penetration testing should be conducted to identify vulnerabilities and strengthen the institution's defenses against cyber threats.

Another crucial component of cyber security in educational institutions is raising awareness among students, teachers, and staff about potential cyber threats and best practices for staying safe online. Training programs on how to recognize phishing scams, malware attacks, and social engineering tactics can help prevent data breaches and protect the institution's digital assets.

Furthermore, establishing a multi-layered defense strategy that includes firewalls, antivirus software, intrusion detection systems, and access controls can help fortify the institution's network against cyber attacks. Regular software updates and patches should also be applied to ensure that systems are up-to-date and protected against known vulnerabilities.

In conclusion, cyber security in schools and universities requires a proactive and comprehensive approach to safeguarding sensitive information and protecting against potential cyber threats. By implementing robust data encryption protocols, raising awareness among students and staff, conducting regular security audits, and establishing a multi-layered defense strategy, educational institutions can mitigate the risks of cyber attacks and ensure the safety of their digital assets.

Securing Student Data

In today's digital age, securing student data is more important than ever before. Educational institutions store a vast amount of sensitive information about their students, including personal details, academic records, and financial information. This data is a prime target for cyber attackers looking to steal identities or commit fraud. It is crucial for professionals in the education sector to have a comprehensive strategy in place to protect student data from cyber threats.

One of the first steps in securing student data is to conduct a thorough risk assessment. This involves identifying potential vulnerabilities in the institution's systems and processes that could be exploited by cyber attackers. By understanding where the weaknesses lie, professionals can take proactive measures to strengthen security measures and mitigate the risk of a data breach.

Another important aspect of securing student data is implementing robust security protocols and access controls. This includes encrypting sensitive information, regularly updating software and systems, and restricting access to data on a need-to-know basis. By limiting the number of individuals who have access to student data, professionals can reduce the likelihood of unauthorized access and data breaches.

Training staff and students on cybersecurity best practices is also essential in securing student data. Educating users on how to recognize phishing emails, create strong passwords, and avoid clicking on malicious links can help prevent cyber attacks. By promoting a culture of cybersecurity awareness within the institution, professionals can empower individuals to play an active role in protecting student data.

Lastly, professionals in the education sector should have a response plan in place in the event of a data breach. This plan should outline the steps to take to contain the breach, assess the impact on student data, notify affected individuals, and work towards restoring the integrity of the institution's systems. By being prepared for a cyber attack, professionals can minimize the damage caused and safeguard the trust of students and their families.

Protecting Educational Resources

Protecting educational resources is crucial in today's digital age, where cyber threats are becoming more sophisticated and prevalent. Educational institutions, ranging from schools to universities, are increasingly becoming targets for cyber attacks due to the vast amount of sensitive data they hold. It is essential for professionals in the education sector to have a comprehensive strategy in place to safeguard their resources and ensure the continuity of education in the face of cyber warfare.

One of the first steps in protecting educational resources is to conduct a thorough risk assessment to identify potential vulnerabilities. This involves analyzing the systems and networks used within the institution to understand where weaknesses may lie. By understanding the potential entry points for cyber attackers, professionals can better prioritize their security measures and allocate resources effectively to mitigate risks.

Implementing robust cybersecurity measures is essential in safeguarding educational resources from cyber threats. This includes deploying firewalls, antivirus software, and intrusion detection systems to prevent unauthorized access to sensitive data. Additionally, regular security updates and patches should be applied to ensure that systems are protected against the latest threats. Educating staff and students on cybersecurity best practices is also crucial in preventing human error from compromising the institution's security.

In the event of a cyber attack, professionals in the education sector should have a response plan in place to minimize the impact on educational resources. This includes establishing communication protocols to ensure that all stakeholders are informed of the situation and taking immediate action to contain the attack. Backing up data regularly and storing it in secure locations is also essential in ensuring that critical educational resources can be recovered in the event of a breach.

Collaboration with other educational institutions and cybersecurity experts is key in staying ahead of cyber threats. By sharing information and best practices, professionals in the education sector can strengthen their defenses and better protect their resources. Investing in ongoing training and professional development for staff is also crucial in building a culture of cybersecurity awareness within the institution. By taking proactive steps to protect educational resources, professionals can ensure that students have access to high-quality education in a secure digital environment.

Chapter 8: Cyber Warfare for Small Businesses

Small Business Cyber Security Risks

Small businesses are increasingly becoming a target for cyber attacks due to their limited resources and lack of robust security measures. As a result, it is crucial for small business owners to understand the cyber security risks they face and take proactive steps to protect their organizations from potential threats.

One of the major cyber security risks facing small businesses is phishing attacks. Phishing involves sending emails or messages that appear to be from a legitimate source in order to trick recipients into providing sensitive information such as login credentials or financial data. Small businesses are particularly vulnerable to phishing attacks because they often lack the sophisticated email filtering systems that larger organizations have in place.

Another common cyber security risk for small businesses is ransomware. Ransomware is a type of malware that encrypts the victim's files and demands a ransom in exchange for the decryption key. Small businesses are attractive targets for ransomware attacks because they are more likely to pay the ransom in order to regain access to their files, making them a profitable target for cyber criminals.

In addition to phishing and ransomware, small businesses also face the risk of data breaches. Data breaches can occur when sensitive information such as customer data or financial records is accessed or stolen by unauthorized individuals. Small businesses are often targeted for data breaches because they typically have weaker security measures in place compared to larger organizations.

To protect against these and other cyber security risks, small business owners should take a proactive approach to cyber security. This includes implementing strong password policies, regularly updating software and systems, training employees on cyber security best practices, and investing in security solutions such as firewalls and antivirus software. By taking these steps, small businesses can reduce their vulnerability to cyber attacks and safeguard their valuable data and assets.

Implementing Cost-Effective Cyber Security Measures

Implementing cost-effective cyber security measures is crucial for professionals in all sectors, especially as cyber warfare becomes an increasing threat in today's digital age. With the rise of sophisticated cyber attacks targeting industries such as healthcare, finance, government, energy, education, small businesses, non-profit organizations, transportation, telecommunications, and defense, it is imperative for professionals to have a solid cyber warfare strategy in place.

One cost-effective measure that professionals can implement is to conduct regular vulnerability assessments and penetration testing. By identifying weaknesses in their systems and networks, organizations can proactively address potential security threats before they are exploited by malicious actors. This proactive approach can help save both time and money in the long run by preventing costly data breaches and downtime.

Another cost-effective cyber security measure is to invest in employee training and awareness programs. Human error remains one of the leading causes of security breaches, so educating employees on best practices for cybersecurity can help mitigate risks. By fostering a culture of security awareness within the organization, professionals can empower their workforce to recognize and respond to potential threats effectively.

Utilizing open-source security tools and resources can also be a cost-effective way to bolster cyber security defenses. Many reputable organizations offer free or low-cost tools that can help professionals monitor their networks, detect anomalies, and respond to incidents promptly. By leveraging these resources, professionals can enhance their cyber security posture without breaking the bank.

Lastly, professionals should consider outsourcing certain aspects of their cyber security operations to managed security service providers (MSSPs). By partnering with experienced MSSPs, organizations can access a team of skilled security experts and cutting-edge technologies without having to invest in costly infrastructure and personnel. This collaborative approach can help professionals stay ahead of emerging threats and ensure that their cyber security measures remain cost-effective and efficient.

Protecting Customer Information

Protecting customer information is a critical aspect of any organization's cyber warfare strategy, regardless of the industry they operate in. In today's digital age, customer data is more valuable than ever, and cyber attackers are constantly looking for ways to exploit vulnerabilities and steal this information for malicious purposes. As professionals, it is our responsibility to take proactive steps to safeguard customer data and prevent unauthorized access.

In the healthcare industry, protecting customer information is especially important due to the sensitive nature of medical records and personal health information. Healthcare organizations must ensure that they have robust security measures in place to prevent data breaches and protect patient privacy. This includes encrypting data, implementing access controls, and regularly auditing systems for vulnerabilities.

Similarly, in the financial sector, safeguarding customer information is paramount to maintaining trust and credibility with clients. Financial institutions must adhere to strict regulations and compliance standards to protect sensitive financial data from cyber threats. This may involve implementing multi-factor authentication, conducting regular security assessments, and educating employees on best practices for data protection.

In the government sector, protecting customer information is crucial for national security and public trust. Government agencies must prioritize cybersecurity measures to defend against cyber attacks and prevent unauthorized access to classified information. This may involve implementing secure networks, conducting regular threat assessments, and collaborating with other agencies to share threat intelligence.

In the energy sector, protecting customer information is essential to ensure the reliability and security of critical infrastructure. Energy companies must implement robust cybersecurity measures to safeguard customer data and prevent disruptions to services. This may involve monitoring networks for suspicious activity, implementing firewalls and intrusion detection systems, and training employees on how to recognize and respond to cyber threats. By prioritizing the protection of customer information, professionals across various industries can strengthen their cyber warfare strategies and defend against evolving threats in the digital landscape.

Chapter 9: Cyber Warfare for Non-Profit Organizations

Cyber Security Challenges for Non-Profits

Non-profit organizations are not immune to the growing threat of cyber warfare. In fact, they are often targeted by cyber criminals due to their lack of resources and expertise in cybersecurity. Non-profits face unique challenges when it comes to protecting their sensitive data and ensuring the security of their networks. This subchapter will explore some of the key cyber security challenges that non-profits must address in order to protect their organizations from cyber attacks.

One of the biggest challenges that non-profits face is limited resources. Many non-profit organizations operate on tight budgets and may not have the financial resources to invest in robust cybersecurity measures. This can leave them vulnerable to cyber attacks, as they may not have the necessary tools and technologies to detect and prevent security breaches. Non-profits must find ways to prioritize cybersecurity within their limited resources in order to protect their sensitive data and maintain the trust of their stakeholders.

Another challenge for non-profits is the lack of cybersecurity expertise. Many non-profit organizations do not have dedicated IT staff or cybersecurity professionals on their team. This means that they may not have the knowledge or skills to effectively defend against cyber attacks. Non-profits must invest in training and education for their staff in order to increase their cybersecurity awareness and build their capacity to respond to security threats.

Non-profits also face the challenge of managing third-party vendors and partners. Many non-profit organizations rely on external vendors for services such as website hosting, payment processing, and donor management. These third-party vendors can introduce security vulnerabilities into the non-profit's network, making them a potential target for cyber attacks. Non-profits must carefully vet their vendors and partners to ensure that they have strong cybersecurity measures in place and are compliant with relevant regulations.

In addition, non-profits must also consider the reputational damage that can result from a cyber attack. Non-profits rely on the trust and support of their donors, volunteers, and stakeholders in order to carry out their missions. A data breach or security incident can erode this trust and damage the organization's reputation, leading to a loss of funding and support. Non-profits must prioritize cybersecurity as a key component of their risk management strategy in order to protect their brand and maintain the confidence of their stakeholders.

Securing Donor Information

In today's digital age, securing donor information is of utmost importance for organizations, especially non-profit organizations that rely on the generosity of donors to support their missions. With cyber warfare becoming increasingly prevalent, it is crucial for professionals in various sectors, including non-profits, to have a comprehensive strategy in place to protect sensitive donor data.

One of the first steps in securing donor information is to implement robust cybersecurity measures to prevent unauthorized access to databases and sensitive information. This includes using encryption technologies to protect data in transit and at rest, as well as implementing multi-factor authentication to ensure that only authorized individuals can access donor information.

Furthermore, regular security audits and vulnerability assessments should be conducted to identify and address any potential weaknesses in the organization's systems. This proactive approach can help prevent data breaches and cyber attacks that could compromise donor information and damage the organization's reputation.

Additionally, it is essential for organizations to educate their staff on best practices for data security, such as avoiding phishing scams and using strong, unique passwords. Human error is often a significant factor in data breaches, so training employees on how to recognize and respond to potential threats can go a long way in protecting donor information.

Finally, organizations should have a response plan in place in the event of a data breach or cyber attack. This plan should outline the steps to take to contain the breach, notify affected donors, and work with law enforcement and cybersecurity experts to investigate the incident. By being prepared and proactive in securing donor information, organizations can mitigate the risks of cyber warfare and protect the trust of their donors.

Protecting Organizational Data

Protecting Organizational Data is crucial in today's digital age where cyber threats are becoming increasingly sophisticated and prevalent. It is imperative for professionals in various industries to have a comprehensive strategy in place to safeguard their sensitive information from cyber attacks. This subchapter will provide guidance on how to plan for cyber warfare in different sectors, including healthcare, finance, government, energy, education, small businesses, non-profit organizations, transportation, telecommunications, and defense.

In the healthcare industry, protecting patient data is paramount to maintaining trust and compliance with regulations such as HIPAA. Professionals in this sector should implement strong encryption protocols, access controls, and regular security audits to prevent unauthorized access to sensitive information. Training staff on cybersecurity best practices is also crucial to mitigate risks posed by human error.

Similarly, in the financial sector, safeguarding customer financial data is essential to prevent fraud and maintain the integrity of financial transactions. Professionals should invest in robust firewalls, intrusion detection systems, and data loss prevention tools to secure their networks. Regularly updating software and conducting vulnerability assessments can help identify and address potential security gaps before they are exploited by cyber attackers.

In the government sector, protecting classified information and critical infrastructure from cyber threats is a top priority. Professionals should collaborate with intelligence agencies and cybersecurity experts to develop comprehensive incident response plans and conduct regular security drills to test the effectiveness of their defenses. Implementing multi-factor authentication and encryption technologies can help prevent unauthorized access to sensitive government data.

In the energy sector, safeguarding operational technology (OT) systems from cyber attacks is essential to prevent disruptions to critical infrastructure such as power plants and utilities. Professionals should implement network segmentation, intrusion detection systems, and continuous monitoring to detect and respond to cyber threats in real-time. Conducting regular penetration testing and threat intelligence sharing with industry peers can help identify and mitigate potential vulnerabilities before they are exploited by malicious actors.

Overall, protecting organizational data requires a multi-layered approach that combines technical safeguards, employee training, and proactive risk management strategies. By staying vigilant and proactive in addressing cyber threats, professionals can effectively mitigate the risks posed by cyber warfare and safeguard their critical assets from unauthorized access and exploitation.

Chapter 10: Cyber Warfare in the Transportation Industry

Cyber Threats to Transportation Systems

Cyber threats to transportation systems are a growing concern in today's digital age. With the increasing reliance on technology to operate transportation networks, the potential for cyber attacks has become a significant risk. From traffic control systems to airline reservation systems, transportation infrastructure is vulnerable to a wide range of cyber threats that could have devastating consequences.

One of the primary cyber threats to transportation systems is the potential for hackers to gain unauthorized access to critical infrastructure. This could include disrupting traffic signals, sabotaging railway systems, or even taking control of autonomous vehicles. The implications of such an attack could be catastrophic, leading to accidents, delays, and even loss of life.

Another major concern is the potential for cyber attacks to disrupt communication systems within transportation networks. This could impact the ability of operators to coordinate and respond to emergencies, leading to confusion and chaos in the event of a crisis. Without reliable communication channels, transportation systems are vulnerable to breakdowns and disruptions that could have far-reaching consequences.

In addition to direct attacks on transportation infrastructure, there is also the threat of cyber espionage targeting sensitive information related to transportation networks. From passenger data to flight schedules, hackers could use stolen information to gain a competitive advantage or even launch further attacks on the transportation industry.

To address these cyber threats, professionals in the transportation industry must prioritize cybersecurity measures to protect their systems and data. This includes implementing robust encryption protocols, regularly updating software and security patches, and conducting regular audits to identify and address vulnerabilities. By taking proactive steps to secure their networks, transportation professionals can help safeguard against cyber attacks and ensure the safety and reliability of their systems.

Securing Transportation Networks

Securing transportation networks is crucial in today's world where cyber warfare is a looming threat. As professionals in the transportation industry, it is imperative to have a comprehensive strategy in place to protect critical infrastructure from cyber attacks. Cyber warfare can disrupt the operations of transportation networks, leading to chaos and potential safety hazards for passengers and goods. Therefore, it is essential to stay ahead of potential threats and have robust security measures in place.

One of the first steps in securing transportation networks is to conduct a thorough risk assessment. This involves identifying potential vulnerabilities in the system and developing a plan to mitigate these risks. Professionals in the transportation industry should work closely with cybersecurity experts to identify weak points in the network and implement necessary safeguards to protect against cyber attacks. By understanding the potential threats facing transportation networks, professionals can better prepare for and defend against potential attacks.

Another important aspect of securing transportation networks is to establish clear protocols and procedures for responding to cyber attacks. Professionals should have a well-defined incident response plan in place to minimize the impact of an attack and quickly restore operations. This plan should outline roles and responsibilities, communication protocols, and steps to contain and remediate the attack. By having a well-prepared response plan, professionals can effectively mitigate the damage caused by cyber attacks and ensure the continuity of transportation services.

In addition to having robust security measures in place, professionals in the transportation industry should also invest in cybersecurity training for employees. By educating staff on best practices for cybersecurity and raising awareness about potential threats, transportation networks can strengthen their defenses against cyber attacks. Training programs should cover topics such as phishing awareness, password security, and incident response procedures to ensure that employees are well-equipped to handle potential threats.

Overall, securing transportation networks requires a proactive approach to cybersecurity and a commitment to protecting critical infrastructure from cyber threats. By conducting risk assessments, developing incident response plans, and providing cybersecurity training for employees, professionals in the transportation industry can strengthen their defenses against cyber attacks and ensure the safety and reliability of transportation networks. It is essential for professionals in the transportation industry to stay vigilant and continuously update their security measures to adapt to evolving cyber threats.

Protecting Passenger Information

Protecting passenger information is crucial in the transportation industry, as cyber threats continue to evolve and pose risks to both individuals and organizations. In order to safeguard sensitive data, professionals must implement comprehensive strategies to mitigate potential attacks and breaches. This subchapter will explore key tactics and best practices for protecting passenger information in the face of cyber warfare.

One of the first steps in protecting passenger information is to establish a robust cybersecurity framework that addresses potential vulnerabilities and threats. This includes conducting regular risk assessments, implementing strong access controls, and ensuring data encryption protocols are in place. By proactively identifying and addressing security gaps, professionals can better protect passenger information from unauthorized access and exploitation.

In addition to technical safeguards, professionals in the transportation industry must also prioritize employee training and awareness programs. Human error remains a significant factor in data breaches, so educating staff on cybersecurity best practices and protocols is essential. This includes providing training on how to recognize phishing attempts, avoid malicious links, and secure sensitive information.

Furthermore, professionals should consider implementing multi-factor authentication and biometric security measures to enhance the protection of passenger information. By requiring additional verification steps beyond passwords, organizations can reduce the risk of unauthorized access and strengthen overall cybersecurity defenses. Biometric security, such as fingerprint or facial recognition, can also provide an added layer of protection against identity theft and fraud.

Ultimately, protecting passenger information requires a proactive and multi-faceted approach that addresses both technical vulnerabilities and human factors. By implementing strong cybersecurity frameworks, conducting regular risk assessments, and prioritizing employee training, professionals in the transportation industry can better safeguard sensitive data from cyber threats and ensure the safety and security of passengers.

Chapter 11: Cyber Warfare in the Telecommunications Sector

Telecommunications Cyber Security Risks

In today's interconnected world, the telecommunications sector plays a critical role in our daily lives. From phone calls to internet access, telecommunications companies are responsible for keeping us connected. However, with this reliance on technology comes the increased risk of cyber attacks. Telecommunications cyber security risks are a major concern for professionals in this industry, as they can have far-reaching consequences for both businesses and individuals.

One of the primary cyber security risks in the telecommunications sector is the threat of data breaches. With the vast amounts of sensitive information that telecommunications companies handle, including personal and financial data, they are a prime target for hackers looking to steal this valuable information. A data breach can have serious repercussions, including financial losses, damage to a company's reputation, and potential legal consequences.

Another major risk in the telecommunications sector is the threat of network disruption. Cyber attacks aimed at disrupting telecommunications networks can result in widespread outages, leaving customers without access to essential services. This can have a significant impact on businesses that rely on telecommunications services to operate, as well as on individuals who depend on these services for communication and connectivity.

Telecommunications companies also face the risk of espionage and sabotage from cyber attackers. Hackers may target telecommunications networks in order to gather intelligence or disrupt operations for political or economic gain. This type of cyber warfare can have serious implications for national security, as well as for the businesses and individuals that rely on telecommunications services.

To address these cyber security risks, professionals in the telecommunications sector must prioritize the implementation of robust security measures. This includes regular monitoring of networks for any unusual activity, implementing strong encryption protocols to protect data, and ensuring that employees are trained in cyber security best practices. By taking proactive steps to safeguard their networks and data, telecommunications companies can reduce the risk of falling victim to cyber attacks and protect both their business and their customers.

Securing Communication Networks

In the realm of cyber warfare, securing communication networks is crucial for professionals in various industries. Whether in the healthcare, financial, government, energy, education, transportation, telecommunications, defense, small business, or non-profit sectors, the ability to protect sensitive information and prevent cyber attacks is paramount. Without a secure communication network, organizations are vulnerable to data breaches, espionage, and sabotage.

One of the first steps in securing communication networks is to implement strong encryption protocols. This ensures that data transmitted over the network is encrypted and secure from prying eyes. Professionals must also regularly update their encryption protocols to keep up with evolving cyber threats and vulnerabilities.

In addition to encryption, professionals should also implement multi-factor authentication to verify the identity of users accessing the network. By requiring multiple forms of authentication, such as passwords, biometrics, or security tokens, organizations can further protect their communication networks from unauthorized access.

Furthermore, professionals should establish strict access controls to limit who can access sensitive information on the network. By segmenting the network and restricting access to certain users or devices, organizations can reduce the risk of insider threats and unauthorized access.

Lastly, professionals should conduct regular security audits and penetration testing to identify and address vulnerabilities in their communication networks. By proactively testing for weaknesses and patching any vulnerabilities, organizations can stay one step ahead of cyber attackers and protect their critical infrastructure from potential threats. By following these best practices for securing communication networks, professionals can better prepare for cyber warfare and safeguard their organizations from potential threats.

Protecting Customer Privacy

Protecting customer privacy is a critical aspect of any organization's cyber warfare strategy. In today's digital age, where personal information is constantly being collected and stored, it is more important than ever to ensure that this data is kept secure from malicious actors. Failure to protect customer privacy can not only result in financial losses due to data breaches, but also damage the reputation and trust of the organization.

One of the key steps in protecting customer privacy is to implement strong encryption protocols. Encryption is a method of encoding information so that only authorized parties can access it. By encrypting sensitive customer data such as personal information, financial records, and passwords, organizations can prevent unauthorized access and protect their customers' privacy.

Another important aspect of protecting customer privacy is to regularly update and patch software and systems. Cyber attackers often exploit vulnerabilities in outdated software to gain access to sensitive information. By keeping software up to date and promptly applying patches, organizations can reduce the risk of data breaches and protect customer privacy.

In addition to encryption and software updates, organizations should also implement strong access controls and authentication mechanisms. Access controls limit the ability of unauthorized users to access sensitive information, while strong authentication mechanisms such as multi-factor authentication can help verify the identity of users and prevent unauthorized access to customer data.

Overall, protecting customer privacy should be a top priority for organizations in all sectors, from healthcare and finance to government and education. By implementing strong encryption protocols, regularly updating software, and implementing access controls and authentication mechanisms, organizations can protect customer privacy and safeguard their reputation and trust.

Chapter 12: Cyber Warfare in the Defense Industry

Military Cyber Threats

Military cyber threats pose a significant risk to national security and are a growing concern for professionals across various industries. As technology advances, so do the capabilities of malicious actors seeking to exploit vulnerabilities in critical infrastructure. In this subchapter, we will explore the unique challenges and strategies for planning for cyber warfare in the military sector.

One of the primary threats facing the military is the potential for cyber attacks on command and control systems. These systems are essential for coordinating military operations and communicating vital information to troops in the field. A successful cyber attack on these systems could disrupt operations, compromise sensitive data, and even lead to physical harm to personnel. Professionals in the military sector must prioritize the security of these systems and develop robust defenses to mitigate the risk of cyber attacks.

Another key concern for the military is the threat of cyber espionage. Foreign adversaries may seek to infiltrate military networks to gather intelligence on troop movements, weapon capabilities, and strategic plans. Professionals in the defense industry must be vigilant in detecting and thwarting these espionage attempts, as the consequences of a security breach could be catastrophic.

In addition to external threats, the military must also contend with insider threats from disgruntled employees or contractors with access to sensitive information. Professionals in the military sector must implement strict access controls, monitor network activity for suspicious behavior, and conduct regular security training to ensure that all personnel are aware of the risks posed by insider threats.

Overall, the military must adopt a multi-layered approach to cybersecurity, incorporating technological solutions, employee training, and proactive threat intelligence to defend against cyber attacks. By staying ahead of emerging threats and continuously improving their security posture, professionals in the military sector can better protect national security and ensure the safety of personnel and assets.

Securing Defense Networks

Securing Defense Networks is a critical aspect of preparing for cyber warfare, especially in the defense industry. With the increasing sophistication of cyber threats, it is essential for professionals in this sector to have robust defense mechanisms in place to protect sensitive information and infrastructure from potential attacks. This subchapter will explore key strategies and best practices for securing defense networks in the face of evolving cyber threats.

One of the first steps in securing defense networks is to conduct a thorough risk assessment to identify potential vulnerabilities and threats. This involves evaluating the current state of the network, identifying potential entry points for attackers, and assessing the potential impact of a successful cyber attack. By understanding the risks facing the network, professionals can develop a targeted defense strategy to mitigate these risks and protect critical assets.

In addition to conducting a risk assessment, professionals in the defense industry should also implement a multi-layered defense strategy to protect their networks. This includes deploying firewalls, intrusion detection systems, and encryption technologies to monitor and secure network traffic, as well as implementing access controls and user authentication mechanisms to prevent unauthorized access to sensitive information. By layering these defense mechanisms, professionals can create a more resilient and secure network that is better equipped to defend against cyber threats.

Another important aspect of securing defense networks is to stay informed about the latest cyber threats and trends. By monitoring industry reports, threat intelligence feeds, and security alerts, professionals can stay one step ahead of potential attackers and proactively address emerging threats before they become a serious problem. This proactive approach to cybersecurity can help professionals in the defense industry anticipate and respond to cyber threats more effectively, ultimately reducing the risk of a successful attack on their networks.

Ultimately, securing defense networks requires a combination of proactive planning, robust defense mechanisms, and ongoing monitoring and assessment. By taking a comprehensive approach to cybersecurity and staying informed about the latest threats, professionals in the defense industry can better protect their networks and ensure the security of critical assets and infrastructure. With cyber warfare posing an ever-increasing threat to national security, it is essential for professionals in this sector to prioritize the security of their networks and take proactive steps to defend against potential attacks.

Protecting Classified Information

Protecting classified information is a critical aspect of any organization's cyber warfare strategy. Whether you work in the healthcare industry, financial sector, government sector, energy sector, education sector, transportation industry, or any other sector, safeguarding sensitive data is essential to prevent cyber attacks and maintain operational security. In this subchapter, we will discuss best practices for protecting classified information and minimizing the risk of data breaches.

One of the first steps in protecting classified information is to establish clear policies and procedures for handling sensitive data. This includes defining what constitutes classified information, who has access to it, and how it should be stored and transmitted. By clearly outlining these guidelines, organizations can ensure that employees understand their responsibilities when it comes to protecting sensitive data.

In addition to establishing policies and procedures, organizations should also invest in secure technology solutions to safeguard classified information. This may include encryption tools, access controls, and secure communication channels. By implementing these technologies, organizations can reduce the risk of data breaches and unauthorized access to sensitive information.

Regular training and awareness programs are also essential for protecting classified information. Employees should be educated on the importance of data security, how to identify potential threats, and what steps to take in the event of a security incident. By keeping employees informed and engaged, organizations can create a culture of cybersecurity awareness that helps prevent data breaches.

Finally, organizations should conduct regular audits and assessments of their data security measures to identify vulnerabilities and areas for improvement. By regularly reviewing and updating their cybersecurity practices, organizations can stay ahead of emerging threats and ensure that their classified information remains secure. Protecting classified information requires a proactive and comprehensive approach that involves policies, technology, training, and ongoing assessment. By following these best practices, organizations can minimize the risk of data breaches and protect their sensitive data from cyber threats.

Chapter 13: Conclusion and Future Trends in Cyber Warfare Strategy

Recap of Cyber Warfare Strategy

In this subchapter, we will provide a recap of the key strategies outlined in this book for professionals to effectively plan for cyber warfare. Cyber warfare is a growing threat in today's digital age, and it is crucial for organizations in various sectors to be prepared for potential cyber attacks.

One of the first steps in planning for cyber warfare is to conduct a thorough risk assessment. This involves identifying potential vulnerabilities in your organization's systems and networks, as well as understanding the potential impact of a cyber attack. By understanding your organization's weaknesses, you can better prioritize resources and efforts to strengthen your defenses.

Another key strategy is to develop a comprehensive incident response plan. This plan should outline the steps to take in the event of a cyber attack, including how to detect, contain, and mitigate the impact of the attack. Having a well-defined incident response plan can help minimize the damage caused by a cyber attack and ensure a swift recovery.

Furthermore, it is important for professionals to stay informed about the latest cyber threats and trends. By staying up-to-date on emerging threats, organizations can proactively adapt their cybersecurity strategies to address new challenges. This may involve investing in new technologies, training employees on best practices, and collaborating with other organizations to share threat intelligence.

Overall, planning for cyber warfare requires a proactive and holistic approach. By conducting risk assessments, developing incident response plans, staying informed about emerging threats, and collaborating with others in the industry, professionals can better prepare their organizations for the ever-evolving landscape of cyber warfare. It is essential for professionals in all sectors, including healthcare, finance, government, energy, education, small businesses, non-profit organizations, transportation, telecommunications, and defense, to prioritize cybersecurity and take proactive steps to protect their assets and data from cyber threats.

Emerging Trends in Cyber Security

In the ever-evolving landscape of cyber warfare, professionals must stay vigilant and adapt to emerging trends in cyber security. As technology advances, so do the tactics used by malicious actors to infiltrate systems and steal data. It is crucial for professionals in various industries to understand the current trends in cyber security to effectively plan and defend against potential cyber attacks.

One emerging trend in cyber security is the rise of ransomware attacks. These attacks involve hackers encrypting a victim's data and demanding a ransom in exchange for the decryption key. Ransomware attacks have become increasingly common in recent years, targeting businesses of all sizes and industries. Professionals must have robust backup and recovery plans in place to mitigate the impact of a ransomware attack and prevent data loss.

Another trend to watch out for is the proliferation of Internet of Things (IoT) devices. These devices, such as smart thermostats and security cameras, are often connected to the internet and vulnerable to cyber attacks. Professionals must ensure that IoT devices are properly secured and regularly updated to prevent hackers from exploiting vulnerabilities to gain access to sensitive information.

Additionally, professionals should be aware of the growing threat of insider attacks. These attacks involve individuals within an organization intentionally or unintentionally compromising security measures to access confidential information. It is essential for professionals to implement strict access controls and monitor user activity to detect and prevent insider threats.

Lastly, professionals should be prepared for the increasing use of artificial intelligence (AI) in cyber attacks. Hackers are leveraging AI technology to automate and streamline their attacks, making them more sophisticated and difficult to detect. Professionals must develop AI-powered defense mechanisms to stay one step ahead of cyber criminals and protect their systems from advanced AI-driven attacks. By staying informed and proactive, professionals can effectively plan for cyber warfare and safeguard their organizations from evolving cyber threats.

Recommendations for Professionals in Cyber Warfare

In order to effectively plan for cyber warfare, professionals in various industries must take proactive measures to protect their organizations from potential cyber threats. One key recommendation for professionals is to establish a comprehensive cybersecurity strategy that includes regular risk assessments, employee training, and incident response plans. By identifying potential vulnerabilities and developing a plan to mitigate risks, organizations can better protect themselves from cyber attacks.

For professionals in the healthcare industry, it is crucial to prioritize the security of patient information and medical records. Healthcare organizations should invest in robust cybersecurity measures, such as encryption and access controls, to prevent unauthorized access to sensitive data. Additionally, regular security audits and employee training programs can help healthcare professionals stay ahead of emerging cyber threats.

Professionals in the financial sector must also prioritize cybersecurity to protect sensitive financial information and prevent fraud. Implementing multi-factor authentication, monitoring for suspicious activity, and regularly updating security systems are key recommendations for professionals in the financial industry. By staying vigilant and proactive in their cybersecurity efforts, financial organizations can reduce the risk of data breaches and financial losses.

In the government sector, professionals must be proactive in defending against cyber threats that could compromise national security. Collaborating with cybersecurity experts, implementing strong encryption protocols, and investing in advanced threat detection technologies are crucial recommendations for professionals in the government sector. By taking a comprehensive approach to cybersecurity, government organizations can better protect critical infrastructure and sensitive government data.

For professionals in the energy, education, transportation, telecommunications, defense, small business, and non-profit sectors, similar recommendations apply. It is essential for professionals in all industries to prioritize cybersecurity, invest in the latest technologies, and stay informed about emerging cyber threats. By following these recommendations and developing a proactive cybersecurity strategy, professionals can better protect their organizations from cyber attacks and safeguard sensitive information.

Case Studies of Notable Cyber Warfare Incidents

Stuxnet:

Introduction Stuxnet is a sophisticated and highly complex computer worm that was discovered in June 2010. It is widely regarded as the first known cyber weapon, designed specifically to target industrial control systems (ICS), particularly those used in Iran's nuclear program. Stuxnet represents a significant evolution in the realm of cyber warfare due to its targeted approach and the implications it had on global cybersecurity practices.

Discovery and Background Stuxnet was first identified by VirusBlokAda, a Belarusian cybersecurity firm, and subsequently analyzed by various cybersecurity experts worldwide. It garnered significant attention due to its unique and complex design, which was far more advanced than typical malware.

Technical Composition Stuxnet is notable for its use of multiple zero-day exploits, rootkits, and a modular structure. Key components include:

1. **Zero-Day Vulnerabilities**: Stuxnet exploited four zero-day vulnerabilities in Windows operating systems, which were previously unknown and unpatched by Microsoft.
2. **Propagation Mechanisms**: The worm spread through USB drives and network shares, leveraging Windows vulnerabilities to infect new systems.

3. **Rootkit Technology**: Stuxnet employed rootkit techniques to hide its presence on infected systems, making detection and removal challenging.
4. **Modular Design**: The malware was designed to update itself and adapt to different environments, indicating a high level of sophistication and planning.

Target and Payload Stuxnet specifically targeted Siemens Step7 software and programmable logic controllers (PLCs) used in industrial environments. Its primary objective was to sabotage Iran's uranium enrichment process by:

1. **Manipulating Centrifuges**: The worm altered the operation of centrifuges at Iran's Natanz facility, causing them to spin at speeds that would damage the equipment while reporting normal operations to monitoring systems.
2. **Attack Vector**: Stuxnet sought out specific configurations of Siemens PLCs connected to frequency converters, which controlled the centrifuges' speed. It modified these settings to cause mechanical stress and eventual failure.

Impact and Implications The Stuxnet attack had significant implications, both technically and politically:

1. **Technical Impact**: Stuxnet successfully damaged approximately 1,000 centrifuges at the Natanz facility, setting back Iran's nuclear program by several years.

2. **Political and Strategic Impact**: The attack is believed to have been a joint operation by the United States and Israel, though neither country has officially confirmed involvement. It demonstrated the potential of cyber weapons to achieve strategic objectives without direct military confrontation.
3. **Cybersecurity Lessons**: Stuxnet highlighted the vulnerabilities in industrial control systems and the need for enhanced cybersecurity measures in critical infrastructure. It prompted governments and organizations to reevaluate their cybersecurity strategies and defenses.

Legacy and Evolution Stuxnet's discovery marked a turning point in cybersecurity, leading to increased awareness of the threats posed by cyber weapons. It has influenced the development of subsequent malware and cyber defense strategies, with key lessons including:

1. **Importance of Patch Management**: The need to address vulnerabilities promptly and maintain updated systems.
2. **Enhanced Monitoring and Detection**: The necessity of advanced monitoring tools to detect sophisticated threats.
3. **Collaboration and Information Sharing**: Encouraging collaboration between governments, private sector entities, and international organizations to share threat intelligence and best practices.

Conclusion Stuxnet is a landmark in the history of cyber warfare, demonstrating the potential for cyber attacks to achieve geopolitical objectives and disrupt critical infrastructure. Its discovery has led to significant advancements in cybersecurity practices and an increased focus on protecting industrial control systems from similar threats. The legacy of Stuxnet continues to influence the field of cybersecurity, underscoring the need for vigilance and innovation in the face of evolving cyber threats.

SolarWinds Attack:

Introduction The SolarWinds attack, also known as the SolarWinds cyberattack, was a major cyber espionage campaign that was discovered in December 2020. It involved the compromise of the software supply chain of SolarWinds, a leading IT management company, and affected numerous high-profile organizations, including U.S. government agencies and Fortune 500 companies. The attack is attributed to a sophisticated nation-state actor, widely believed to be the Russian intelligence agency SVR, also known as APT29 or Cozy Bear.

Discovery and Background The attack was first publicly disclosed by cybersecurity firm FireEye, which detected a breach in its own systems and traced the intrusion back to SolarWinds' Orion software. SolarWinds' Orion is a network management product used by thousands of organizations worldwide.

Technical Composition The SolarWinds attack was notable for its complexity and stealth. Key components include:

1. **Supply Chain Compromise**: The attackers infiltrated SolarWinds' software build system and inserted malicious code into updates of the Orion software, distributed between March and June 2020.
2. **SUNBURST Backdoor**: The malicious code, dubbed SUNBURST, created a backdoor on affected systems, allowing attackers to remotely access and control the compromised networks.
3. **TEARDROP and RAINDROP Malware**: Once inside the network, the attackers used additional malware, such as TEARDROP and

RAINDROP, to maintain persistence, escalate privileges, and move laterally across the network.

4. **Stealth and Evasion Techniques**: The attackers employed sophisticated techniques to evade detection, including the use of legitimate network protocols and stolen credentials, as well as delaying activation of the backdoor to avoid raising suspicion.

Impact and Implications The SolarWinds attack had far-reaching consequences, both in terms of its immediate impact and broader implications:

1. **Affected Organizations**: Over 18,000 SolarWinds customers received the compromised updates. High-profile victims included U.S. federal agencies (such as the Department of Homeland Security, Treasury, and Commerce), state and local governments, and numerous private sector companies.
2. **Data Exfiltration**: The primary objective of the attack appeared to be espionage, with attackers exfiltrating sensitive data from targeted organizations. The full extent of the data theft remains unknown.
3. **Supply Chain Vulnerabilities**: The attack highlighted the vulnerabilities inherent in software supply chains, demonstrating how a single compromised vendor can have a cascading effect on multiple organizations.
4. **National Security Implications**: The breach had significant national security implications, prompting the U.S. government to take action, including sanctions against Russia and a comprehensive review of federal cybersecurity practices.

Response and Mitigation The response to the SolarWinds attack involved coordinated efforts from multiple entities:

1. **Incident Response**: Organizations affected by the breach undertook extensive incident response measures, including isolating affected systems, conducting forensic investigations, and implementing remediation actions.
2. **Government Actions**: The U.S. government issued emergency directives to mitigate the impact of the breach and initiated efforts to enhance cybersecurity across federal agencies.
3. **Industry Collaboration**: Cybersecurity firms and industry groups collaborated to analyze the attack, share intelligence, and develop detection and mitigation tools. Notable contributions came from companies like Microsoft, FireEye, and CISA (Cybersecurity and Infrastructure Security Agency).

Lessons Learned The SolarWinds attack underscored several critical lessons for cybersecurity:

1. **Supply Chain Security**: The importance of securing software supply chains and conducting thorough security assessments of third-party vendors.
2. **Zero Trust Architecture**: The need to adopt a zero-trust approach to security, assuming that breaches are inevitable and implementing strict access controls and continuous monitoring.
3. **Advanced Threat Detection**: The necessity of investing in advanced threat detection and response capabilities to identify and mitigate sophisticated attacks.

4. **Collaboration and Information Sharing**: The value of collaboration between public and private sectors to enhance threat intelligence and coordinate responses to cyber incidents.

Conclusion The SolarWinds attack represents a landmark event in the realm of cybersecurity, demonstrating the potential impact of supply chain compromises and the capabilities of nation-state actors. It has led to increased awareness and investment in cybersecurity measures, with a focus on securing supply chains, adopting zero-trust architectures, and enhancing detection and response capabilities. The lessons learned from this attack continue to shape cybersecurity strategies and practices globally.

NotPetya:

Introduction NotPetya, also known as Petya or Nyetya, is a destructive malware attack that occurred on June 27, 2017. Initially perceived as ransomware due to its demand for a ransom payment in Bitcoin, it soon became clear that NotPetya's primary purpose was to cause widespread disruption and damage rather than to generate profit. It targeted organizations worldwide but had a particularly devastating impact on businesses in Ukraine.

Discovery and Background NotPetya was first observed spreading rapidly across various networks, encrypting files and rendering systems inoperable. The attack appeared to be a variant of the Petya ransomware, which had been active since 2016. However, NotPetya's characteristics and behavior distinguished it as a highly destructive cyber weapon rather than a conventional ransomware attack.

Technical Composition NotPetya utilized a combination of sophisticated techniques to propagate and cause damage:

1. **Propagation Mechanisms**: The malware spread using multiple methods:
    - **EternalBlue Exploit**: Leveraged the EternalBlue exploit, which had been previously used in the WannaCry ransomware attack, to target a vulnerability in Microsoft Windows' Server Message Block (SMB) protocol.
    - **EternalRomance Exploit**: Another exploit targeting SMB vulnerabilities.

- **PsExec and WMI**: Used legitimate Windows tools (PsExec and Windows Management Instrumentation) to spread within networks, exploiting stolen credentials.
2. **Encryption and Destruction**: Unlike traditional ransomware, NotPetya's encryption was designed to be irreversible:
    - **Master Boot Record (MBR) Overwrite**: The malware overwrote the MBR, making the system unbootable.
    - **File Encryption**: It encrypted files on the infected systems, but the decryption key was not recoverable, making data restoration impossible even if the ransom was paid.
3. **Ransom Note**: Displayed a ransom note demanding payment in Bitcoin to recover encrypted files. However, paying the ransom did not lead to data recovery, as the attack's primary goal was to cause disruption.

Impact and Implications The NotPetya attack had a significant impact on organizations globally, with Ukraine being the most affected:

1. **Affected Organizations**: Major corporations, government agencies, and critical infrastructure in Ukraine were hit, including banks, airports, and utilities. Internationally, companies like Maersk, Merck, FedEx, and others experienced severe disruptions.
2. **Economic Damage**: The financial cost of the attack was enormous, with estimates of damages exceeding $10 billion. Companies faced substantial losses due to operational disruptions, data loss, and recovery efforts.
3. **Geopolitical Context**: The attack is widely attributed to a Russian state-sponsored group, and it was perceived as part of a broader

cyber campaign against Ukraine, coinciding with ongoing geopolitical tensions between Russia and Ukraine.

Response and Mitigation The response to NotPetya involved extensive efforts to contain the spread and recover from the attack:

1. **Incident Response**: Organizations affected by the attack engaged in large-scale incident response efforts, including isolating infected systems, restoring backups, and rebuilding IT infrastructure.
2. **Patching and Security Updates**: The attack highlighted the importance of timely application of security patches and updates to mitigate known vulnerabilities.
3. **Improved Cyber Hygiene**: Emphasized the need for robust cybersecurity practices, including network segmentation, multi-factor authentication, and regular security audits.

Lessons Learned NotPetya provided several critical lessons for the cybersecurity community:

1. **Supply Chain Security**: The initial infection vector for NotPetya was a compromised update to a popular Ukrainian accounting software, MEDoc. This underscored the importance of securing the software supply chain and verifying the integrity of software updates.
2. **Comprehensive Incident Response Plans**: The attack demonstrated the need for organizations to have comprehensive and tested incident response plans in place to quickly address and mitigate the impact of cyber attacks.

3. **Resilience and Recovery**: Highlighted the importance of having robust backup and recovery strategies to restore operations and minimize downtime in the event of a cyber incident.
4. **International Cooperation**: Stressed the necessity for international cooperation and information sharing among governments, private sector entities, and cybersecurity organizations to effectively combat cyber threats.

Conclusion NotPetya stands out as one of the most destructive cyber attacks in history, primarily due to its intent to cause widespread disruption and its sophisticated propagation mechanisms. The attack served as a wake-up call for organizations worldwide, emphasizing the critical need for robust cybersecurity measures, timely patch management, and comprehensive incident response strategies. The lessons learned from NotPetya continue to influence cybersecurity practices and policies, shaping efforts to defend against future cyber threats.

The Sony Pictures Hack:

Introduction The Sony Pictures hack, also known as the Guardians of Peace (GOP) hack, was a significant cyber attack on Sony Pictures Entertainment (SPE) that took place in late November 2014. The attack resulted in the theft and release of vast amounts of confidential data, causing substantial financial and reputational damage to the company. The hack is widely attributed to the North Korean hacker group known as the Lazarus Group.

Discovery and Background The attack was first discovered on November 24, 2014, when employees of Sony Pictures Entertainment saw a message on their computer screens saying that the company's network had been hacked by the "Guardians of Peace." The hackers had infiltrated Sony's network weeks before the attack was discovered and had exfiltrated a massive amount of data.

Technical Composition The Sony Pictures hack involved several sophisticated techniques:

1. **Spear-Phishing**: The attackers used spear-phishing emails to gain initial access to Sony's network. These emails were carefully crafted to deceive recipients into clicking on malicious links or attachments.
2. **Malware Deployment**: Once inside the network, the attackers deployed malware, including the destructive wiper malware known as "Destover," which was designed to erase data on infected systems.

3. **Data Exfiltration**: The attackers stole terabytes of data, including emails, financial records, confidential documents, and unreleased films.
4. **Public Release**: The stolen data was gradually released to the public, causing significant embarrassment and operational disruption to Sony Pictures.

Impact and Implications The impact of the Sony Pictures hack was far-reaching and multifaceted:

1. **Data Breach**: Sensitive information, including personal data of employees, internal emails, financial information, and intellectual property, was leaked. This included embarrassing email exchanges between executives, details of employee salaries, and unreleased movies.
2. **Financial Costs**: The breach resulted in substantial financial losses for Sony Pictures due to the disruption of business operations, costs of remediation, legal expenses, and loss of intellectual property.
3. **Reputational Damage**: The leaked emails and documents caused significant reputational damage to Sony Pictures and its executives. The hack also led to strained relationships with talent and partners.
4. **Political Ramifications**: The attack was linked to North Korea in retaliation for the planned release of "The Interview," a satirical film about a plot to assassinate North Korean leader Kim Jong-un. This led to heightened tensions between the U.S. and North Korea.

Response and Mitigation Sony Pictures and various stakeholders took several steps in response to the hack:

1. **Incident Response**: Sony Pictures engaged cybersecurity firms to assist in the incident response, containment, and remediation efforts. This included isolating infected systems, restoring from backups, and strengthening security measures.
2. **Government Involvement**: The U.S. government became involved, with the FBI attributing the attack to North Korea. President Obama announced that the U.S. would respond proportionally to the cyber attack.
3. **Public Relations**: Sony Pictures undertook a significant public relations effort to manage the fallout from the leaked information and to reassure stakeholders.

Lessons Learned The Sony Pictures hack highlighted several key lessons for cybersecurity:

1. **Spear-Phishing Awareness**: The importance of educating employees about the dangers of spear-phishing and implementing robust email security measures.
2. **Incident Response Preparedness**: The need for comprehensive incident response plans that include regular drills and readiness for different types of cyber incidents.
3. **Data Encryption and Protection**: Ensuring that sensitive data is encrypted and access is tightly controlled to minimize the impact of data breaches.
4. **International Cybersecurity Cooperation**: The attack underscored the need for international cooperation in responding to and deterring state-sponsored cyber attacks.

Conclusion The Sony Pictures hack remains one of the most high-profile and damaging cyber attacks in history. It demonstrated the potential for cyber attacks to cause significant financial, operational, and reputational damage to organizations. The incident also highlighted the role of state-sponsored cyber warfare in pursuing geopolitical objectives and underscored the need for robust cybersecurity measures, employee awareness, and international cooperation to defend against such threats.

The Office of Personnel Management (OPM) Data Breach:

Introduction The Office of Personnel Management (OPM) data breach, discovered in 2015, is one of the most significant cyber espionage incidents in U.S. history. The breach involved the theft of sensitive personal information of millions of current and former federal employees, contractors, and job applicants. The attack is widely attributed to Chinese state-sponsored hackers.

Discovery and Background The OPM data breach was discovered in April 2015, but further investigations revealed that the intrusion had been ongoing since at least 2014. Two separate breaches were identified: one targeting personnel records and another targeting background investigation data.

Technical Composition The OPM data breach involved a combination of sophisticated cyber espionage techniques:

1. **Initial Compromise**: The attackers initially gained access to OPM's network using stolen credentials. These credentials were likely obtained through spear-phishing attacks or other social engineering techniques.
2. **Advanced Persistent Threat (APT)**: The attackers employed advanced persistent threat (APT) tactics, maintaining a long-term presence in the network to exfiltrate data stealthily over time.
3. **Custom Malware**: The attackers used custom malware, including a variant known as "PlugX," to maintain access, move laterally within the network, and extract data.

4. **Data Exfiltration**: Large volumes of data were exfiltrated, including personnel records and detailed background investigation information stored in the Electronic Questionnaires for Investigations Processing (e-QIP) system.

Impact and Implications The OPM data breach had severe implications for national security, privacy, and cybersecurity:

1. **Scope of the Breach**: The personal information of approximately 21.5 million individuals was compromised. This included Social Security numbers, fingerprints, addresses, health information, and detailed security clearance information.
2. **National Security Risks**: The stolen data included highly sensitive information about individuals with security clearances, potentially exposing them to blackmail, espionage, and other security risks.
3. **Privacy Concerns**: The breach raised significant privacy concerns, as the compromised information included extensive personal details about millions of individuals, including non-government employees who underwent background checks.
4. **Government Response**: The breach prompted widespread criticism of OPM's cybersecurity practices and led to the resignation of OPM's director. The U.S. government undertook efforts to enhance federal cybersecurity practices and improve the protection of sensitive data.

Response and Mitigation The response to the OPM data breach involved multiple steps to address the immediate and long-term impacts:

1. **Notification and Support**: Affected individuals were notified of the breach and offered identity theft protection services, including credit monitoring and identity restoration services.
2. **Incident Response and Investigation**: Federal agencies, including the FBI and DHS, conducted thorough investigations to understand the scope and methods of the breach and to attribute the attack.
3. **Enhanced Cybersecurity Measures**: OPM and other federal agencies implemented enhanced cybersecurity measures, including multi-factor authentication, continuous monitoring, and improved network defenses.
4. **Legislative and Policy Changes**: The breach led to increased scrutiny of federal cybersecurity practices, resulting in legislative and policy changes aimed at strengthening the overall cybersecurity posture of federal agencies.

Lessons Learned The OPM data breach underscored several critical lessons for cybersecurity:

1. **Importance of Credential Security**: The breach highlighted the need for strong authentication mechanisms, including multi-factor authentication, to protect against unauthorized access using stolen credentials.
2. **Comprehensive Security Monitoring**: The necessity of continuous monitoring and advanced threat detection capabilities to identify and respond to persistent threats.
3. **Data Protection and Encryption**: The importance of encrypting sensitive data both at rest and in transit to minimize the impact of data breaches.

4. **Risk Management and Incident Response**: The need for robust risk management practices and well-prepared incident response plans to address and mitigate the effects of cyber incidents.

Conclusion The OPM data breach remains a stark reminder of the vulnerabilities in handling sensitive personal information and the critical importance of robust cybersecurity measures. It highlighted the potential national security risks associated with large-scale data breaches and prompted significant efforts to enhance the cybersecurity resilience of federal agencies. The lessons learned from the OPM data breach continue to influence cybersecurity policies and practices, underscoring the need for vigilance, advanced security measures, and comprehensive risk management strategies.

Frameworks and Standards

NIST Cybersecurity Framework: A Comprehensive Summary

Introduction The National Institute of Standards and Technology (NIST) Cybersecurity Framework (CSF) is a voluntary framework that provides guidelines, best practices, and standards for organizations to manage and reduce cybersecurity risk. Originally published in February 2014 and updated in April 2018 (version 1.1), the framework was developed through collaboration between the U.S. government and private sector. It aims to improve the cybersecurity posture of critical infrastructure and other sectors.

Framework Structure The NIST Cybersecurity Framework is composed of three main components: the Framework Core, Implementation Tiers, and Profiles.

1. **Framework Core** The Framework Core provides a set of desired cybersecurity activities and outcomes using common language that is easy to understand. It consists of five concurrent and continuous Functions, each subdivided into Categories and Subcategories, with informative references to specific standards, guidelines, and practices.
    - **Functions**:
        1. **Identify**: Develop an organizational understanding to manage cybersecurity risk to systems, people, assets, data, and capabilities. Key Categories include Asset Management, Business Environment, Governance, Risk Assessment, and Risk Management Strategy.

2. **Protect**: Develop and implement appropriate safeguards to ensure the delivery of critical services. Key Categories include Identity Management and Access Control, Awareness and Training, Data Security, Information Protection Processes and Procedures, Maintenance, and Protective Technology.
3. **Detect**: Develop and implement appropriate activities to identify the occurrence of a cybersecurity event. Key Categories include Anomalies and Events, Security Continuous Monitoring, and Detection Processes.
4. **Respond**: Develop and implement appropriate activities to take action regarding a detected cybersecurity incident. Key Categories include Response Planning, Communications, Analysis, Mitigation, and Improvements.
5. **Recover**: Develop and implement appropriate activities to maintain plans for resilience and to restore any capabilities or services that were impaired due to a cybersecurity incident. Key Categories include Recovery Planning, Improvements, and Communications.

2. **Implementation Tiers** The Implementation Tiers provide context on how an organization views cybersecurity risk and the processes in place to manage that risk. The Tiers range from Partial (Tier 1) to Adaptive (Tier 4), describing an increasing degree of rigor and sophistication in cybersecurity risk management practices.
    - **Tier 1 (Partial)**: Risk management practices are not formalized and are performed in an ad-hoc, reactive manner.

- **Tier 2 (Risk Informed)**: Risk management practices are approved by management but may not be established as organizational-wide policy.
- **Tier 3 (Repeatable)**: Risk management practices are formally approved, documented, and communicated. They are established as organizational-wide policy.
- **Tier 4 (Adaptive)**: Risk management practices are continuously improving and adapting based on lessons learned and predictive indicators derived from real-time, continuous monitoring.

3. **Profiles** Profiles represent the alignment of an organization's cybersecurity activities with its business requirements, risk tolerance, and resources. They are used to identify and prioritize opportunities for improving cybersecurity posture by comparing a Current Profile (current state) with a Target Profile (desired state).

Benefits and Use Cases The NIST Cybersecurity Framework is designed to be flexible and adaptable, suitable for organizations of all sizes and across various sectors. Key benefits include:

1. **Common Language**: Provides a common language and taxonomy for discussing and managing cybersecurity risk, facilitating communication across all levels of an organization and with external stakeholders.
2. **Risk Management**: Helps organizations prioritize investments and efforts based on risk management principles, enhancing their ability to manage and mitigate cybersecurity risks.

3. **Compliance and Best Practices**: Assists organizations in meeting regulatory and compliance requirements and adopting industry best practices.
4. **Continuous Improvement**: Encourages continuous improvement through regular assessment and adjustment of cybersecurity practices, fostering resilience against evolving threats.

Implementation Steps Organizations can implement the NIST Cybersecurity Framework by following a structured approach:

1. **Prioritize and Scope**: Define the organization's priorities, scope, and critical assets to be protected.
2. **Orient**: Identify the systems, assets, data, and capabilities within the scope, and understand the context, including threats and vulnerabilities.
3. **Create a Current Profile**: Assess the organization's current cybersecurity practices against the Framework Core.
4. **Conduct a Risk Assessment**: Evaluate the risk to the organization's critical assets and operations.
5. **Create a Target Profile**: Define the desired state of cybersecurity capabilities and practices.
6. **Determine, Analyze, and Prioritize Gaps**: Identify gaps between the Current Profile and Target Profile, and prioritize them based on risk and business impact.
7. **Implement Action Plan**: Develop and implement an action plan to address the identified gaps and achieve the Target Profile.

Conclusion The NIST Cybersecurity Framework is a comprehensive and flexible tool that helps organizations enhance their cybersecurity posture by providing a structured approach to managing and reducing cybersecurity risk. By adopting the Framework, organizations can improve their resilience to cyber threats, align cybersecurity activities with business objectives, and foster a culture of continuous improvement in cybersecurity practices.

ISO/IEC 27001: A Comprehensive Summary

Introduction ISO/IEC 27001 is an international standard for managing information security, established by the International Organization for Standardization (ISO) and the International Electrotechnical Commission (IEC). The standard provides a systematic approach to managing sensitive company information so that it remains secure. It covers people, processes, and IT systems by applying a risk management process.

Purpose The main purpose of ISO/IEC 27001 is to provide a framework for establishing, implementing, maintaining, and continuously improving an Information Security Management System (ISMS). An ISMS helps organizations of any size, in any industry, to protect their information systematically and cost-effectively.

Key Components ISO/IEC 27001 is structured into several main components that outline the requirements for an effective ISMS:

1. **Context of the Organization**
    - Understand the organization and its context.
    - Identify interested parties and their requirements.
    - Determine the scope of the ISMS.
    - Establish an ISMS policy.
2. **Leadership**
    - Provide leadership and commitment.
    - Establish an information security policy.
    - Assign roles, responsibilities, and authorities.
3. **Planning**

- Address risks and opportunities.
- Establish information security objectives and plans to achieve them.
- Conduct risk assessments and treatments.

4. **Support**
    - Provide necessary resources.
    - Ensure competence and awareness.
    - Maintain communication and documented information.

5. **Operation**
    - Plan and control ISMS processes.
    - Perform risk assessments and treatments.
    - Manage operational controls.

6. **Performance Evaluation**
    - Monitor, measure, analyze, and evaluate the ISMS.
    - Conduct internal audits.
    - Perform management reviews.

7. **Improvement**
    - Identify and act on nonconformities and corrective actions.
    - Continually improve the ISMS.

Risk Management Process A crucial aspect of ISO/IEC 27001 is its risk management process. This involves:

1. **Risk Assessment**: Identify risks to information security, analyze their potential impact, and evaluate the likelihood of their occurrence.
2. **Risk Treatment**: Decide on measures to mitigate, transfer, avoid, or accept risks. Implement controls to manage or reduce risks to an acceptable level.

Annex A - Control Objectives and Controls Annex A of ISO/IEC 27001 provides a comprehensive list of control objectives and controls, divided into 14 domains:

1. **Information Security Policies**
2. **Organization of Information Security**
3. **Human Resource Security**
4. **Asset Management**
5. **Access Control**
6. **Cryptography**
7. **Physical and Environmental Security**
8. **Operations Security**
9. **Communications Security**
10. **System Acquisition, Development, and Maintenance**
11. **Supplier Relationships**
12. **Information Security Incident Management**
13. **Information Security Aspects of Business Continuity Management**
14. **Compliance**

These controls are not mandatory but serve as a guide to help organizations select appropriate controls based on their risk assessment and treatment plans.

Certification Process Organizations can seek certification to ISO/IEC 27001 to demonstrate their commitment to information security. The certification process involves:

1. **Gap Analysis** (optional): An initial review to identify any gaps between the organization's current practices and the ISO/IEC 27001 requirements.
2. **Stage 1 Audit**: A preliminary audit to review the ISMS documentation and determine readiness for the Stage 2 audit.
3. **Stage 2 Audit**: A comprehensive audit to evaluate the implementation and effectiveness of the ISMS.
4. **Certification**: If the organization passes the Stage 2 audit, it receives ISO/IEC 27001 certification, typically valid for three years.
5. **Surveillance Audits**: Regular audits (usually annual) to ensure ongoing compliance and continual improvement of the ISMS.
6. **Recertification Audit**: Conducted at the end of the three-year certification period to renew the certification.

Benefits Implementing ISO/IEC 27001 provides numerous benefits:

1. **Improved Information Security**: Systematic approach to managing sensitive information and reducing risk.
2. **Compliance**: Helps meet legal, regulatory, and contractual requirements.
3. **Customer Trust**: Demonstrates commitment to security, enhancing customer confidence.
4. **Risk Management**: Identifies and mitigates risks to information security.
5. **Business Continuity**: Enhances the ability to respond to and recover from disruptive incidents.

Conclusion ISO/IEC 27001 is a globally recognized standard for information security management. It provides a robust framework for organizations to manage their information security risks systematically and effectively. By implementing and certifying to ISO/IEC 27001, organizations can protect their sensitive information, comply with legal and regulatory requirements, and build trust with stakeholders.

MITRE ATT&CK Framework: A Comprehensive Summary

Introduction The MITRE ATT&CK (Adversarial Tactics, Techniques, and Common Knowledge) Framework is a globally recognized, detailed knowledge base of adversary tactics and techniques based on real-world observations. Developed by the MITRE Corporation, it is widely used by cybersecurity professionals to understand and counteract cyber threats. ATT&CK provides a common language for describing adversary behavior and a structured approach for enhancing cybersecurity operations.

Purpose The primary purpose of the MITRE ATT&CK Framework is to provide a comprehensive matrix of tactics and techniques that adversaries use during various phases of a cyber attack. It helps organizations understand how attacks are conducted, identify vulnerabilities in their defenses, and develop strategies to detect, respond to, and mitigate cyber threats.

Framework Structure The MITRE ATT&CK Framework is organized into several matrices, each focusing on different domains and aspects of cybersecurity:

1. **ATT&CK for Enterprise**
   - **Tactics**: Represent the adversary's goal or objective at a particular stage of an attack. There are 14 tactics in the Enterprise matrix, including Initial Access, Execution, Persistence, Privilege Escalation, Defense Evasion, Credential Access, Discovery, Lateral Movement, Collection, Command and Control, Exfiltration, and Impact.

- **Techniques**: Specific methods adversaries use to achieve their tactical objectives. Each technique includes detailed descriptions, examples, mitigations, and detection recommendations.
- **Sub-techniques**: More granular actions that further define a technique. They provide additional context and detail.

2. **ATT&CK for Mobile**
   - Focuses on tactics and techniques used by adversaries targeting mobile devices and platforms, such as Android and iOS.

3. **ATT&CK for ICS (Industrial Control Systems)**
   - Addresses tactics and techniques used in attacks against industrial control systems, highlighting the unique challenges and threats in operational technology (OT) environments.

Key Components

1. **Tactics**
   - Broad categories representing adversaries' technical goals during an attack. Examples include:
     - **Initial Access**: Gaining access to the target network.
     - **Execution**: Running malicious code on a target system.
     - **Persistence**: Maintaining a foothold within the network.
     - **Defense Evasion**: Avoiding detection and defensive measures.

2. **Techniques and Sub-techniques**
   - Specific methods used to achieve tactical objectives. Examples include:

- **Phishing (Initial Access)**: Using deceptive emails to gain initial access.
- **PowerShell (Execution)**: Using PowerShell scripts to execute malicious commands.
- **Credential Dumping (Credential Access)**: Extracting credentials from the operating system.

3. **Procedures**
   - Real-world instances of how adversaries have implemented techniques. These are often derived from documented cyber incidents and threat intelligence reports.

Applications and Use Cases

1. **Threat Intelligence**
   - Provides a structured way to collect, analyze, and share threat intelligence, enabling organizations to understand adversary behavior and anticipate future attacks.

2. **Security Operations**
   - Helps in developing and refining detection, investigation, and response capabilities by identifying gaps in security controls and ensuring comprehensive coverage of attack vectors.

3. **Red Teaming and Penetration Testing**
   - Guides the creation of realistic adversary simulations, enabling organizations to test and improve their defenses against tactics and techniques used by real-world attackers.

4. **Compliance and Auditing**

- Assists in mapping security controls to specific tactics and techniques, facilitating compliance with regulatory requirements and security standards.

5. **Risk Management**
    - Enhances risk assessments by providing detailed information on potential attack vectors and their impact, helping organizations prioritize security investments and mitigation strategies.

Benefits

1. **Common Language**: Establishes a standardized vocabulary for describing cyber threats, improving communication and collaboration within and between organizations.
2. **Comprehensive Coverage**: Offers a thorough catalog of adversary behaviors based on real-world observations, providing a deep understanding of the threat landscape.
3. **Actionable Insights**: Includes detailed information on detecting, mitigating, and responding to specific techniques, enabling organizations to improve their security posture.
4. **Continuous Improvement**: Encourages organizations to regularly update and refine their security measures based on the latest threat intelligence and observed adversary behaviors.

Conclusion The MITRE ATT&CK Framework is a powerful tool for cybersecurity professionals, offering a detailed, structured approach to understanding and countering cyber threats. By leveraging the insights provided by ATT&CK, organizations can enhance their threat detection, incident response, and overall cybersecurity resilience. The framework's comprehensive and real-world approach makes it an essential resource for improving cybersecurity strategies and operations across various domains.

CIS Controls: A Comprehensive Summary

Introduction The Center for Internet Security (CIS) Controls, also known as the CIS Critical Security Controls (CIS CSC), is a set of best practices for securing IT systems and data against the most pervasive cyber threats. Developed by the Center for Internet Security, these controls provide a prioritized and actionable path to improve cybersecurity posture for organizations of all sizes.

Purpose The main purpose of the CIS Controls is to provide a framework for organizations to follow to reduce their cyber risk. The controls are designed to be effective against a wide range of attacks and are based on the actual experiences and insights of global cybersecurity experts.

Framework Structure The CIS Controls are organized into three categories: Basic, Foundational, and Organizational. There are 20 controls, each with several sub-controls providing specific actions that organizations can implement.

1. **Basic Controls**
    - These are the essential steps that every organization should take to create a strong foundation for cybersecurity.

    2. **Inventory and Control of Enterprise Assets**: Identify and manage hardware devices connected to the network.
    3. **Inventory and Control of Software Assets**: Identify and manage software applications running on the network.
    4. **Data Protection**: Protect organizational data through proper handling, storage, and access controls.

5. **Secure Configuration of Enterprise Assets and Software**: Maintain security configurations of hardware and software.
6. **Account Management**: Use a formal process to manage the lifecycle of user accounts and access.

2. **Foundational Controls**
    - These controls build on the basic controls and further enhance security.

    6. **Access Control Management**: Implement strong access control policies to limit access to resources based on roles and responsibilities.
    7. **Continuous Vulnerability Management**: Continuously acquire, assess, and take action on information regarding new vulnerabilities.
    8. **Audit Log Management**: Collect, manage, and analyze audit logs to identify potential security incidents.
    9. **Email and Web Browser Protections**: Protect against email and web browser-based attacks.
    10. **Malware Defenses**: Control the installation, spread, and execution of malicious code.
    11. **Data Recovery**: Implement processes to ensure data can be recovered following an incident.
    12. **Network Infrastructure Management**: Secure network infrastructure through proper design, configuration, and segmentation.

13. **Security Awareness and Skills Training**: Conduct regular training for employees to recognize and respond to security threats.

14. **Service Provider Management**: Ensure that third-party service providers adhere to security requirements.

15. **Application Software Security**: Manage the security lifecycle of all in-house and third-party software.

16. **Incident Response Management**: Develop and implement an incident response capability.

3. **Organizational Controls**
   - These controls focus on managing the security program and aligning it with organizational goals.

17. **Security Management**: Establish a security management program.

18. **Security Assessment and Testing**: Regularly test the effectiveness of security controls through assessments and audits.

19. **Secure Network Engineering**: Implement security practices in network design and management.

20. **Penetration Testing**: Conduct penetration tests to identify and address vulnerabilities.

Key Components

1. **Implementation Groups (IGs)**

- The CIS Controls are divided into three Implementation Groups based on organizational size, resources, and cybersecurity maturity.
    - **IG1**: Essential cyber hygiene for small organizations or those with limited resources.
    - **IG2**: Intermediate controls for medium-sized organizations with moderate resources.
    - **IG3**: Advanced controls for large organizations with substantial resources and higher risk exposure.
2. **Safeguards**
    - Each control includes specific safeguards that provide detailed instructions for implementing the control. Safeguards are tailored to different Implementation Groups.

Benefits

1. **Prioritization**: The controls are prioritized, helping organizations focus on the most critical actions to reduce cyber risk.
2. **Actionable Guidance**: Provides clear, specific actions that organizations can take to enhance their cybersecurity.
3. **Adaptability**: Suitable for organizations of all sizes and across various industries.
4. **Alignment with Standards**: Aligns with other major cybersecurity frameworks and standards, facilitating compliance and integration with existing security programs.

Applications and Use Cases

1. **Security Baseline**: Establish a baseline of cybersecurity practices for an organization.
2. **Compliance**: Help meet regulatory requirements and industry standards.
3. **Risk Management**: Identify and mitigate security risks systematically.
4. **Incident Response**: Improve incident response capabilities and readiness.

Conclusion The CIS Controls provide a practical, prioritized approach to cybersecurity that helps organizations of all sizes improve their defenses against cyber threats. By following the CIS Controls, organizations can systematically reduce their risk, enhance their security posture, and protect their critical assets and data. The framework's emphasis on prioritization and actionable guidance makes it an essential tool for any organization's cybersecurity strategy.

Tools and Technologies

SIEM Solutions (Security Information and Event Management): A Comprehensive Summary

Introduction Security Information and Event Management (SIEM) solutions are comprehensive tools designed to provide a holistic view of an organization's information security. They integrate the functions of Security Information Management (SIM) and Security Event Management (SEM) to offer real-time analysis of security alerts generated by applications and network hardware.

Purpose The primary purpose of SIEM solutions is to detect, analyze, and respond to security threats and incidents. They collect and aggregate log data from across the organization's IT infrastructure, enabling centralized management and correlation of security events.

Key Components SIEM solutions comprise several critical components and functionalities:

1. **Data Collection**
    - Collect log and event data from various sources including network devices, servers, databases, applications, and security appliances.
2. **Data Aggregation**
    - Consolidate collected data into a centralized repository, making it easier to manage and analyze.
3. **Normalization**

- Standardize log data from different sources into a common format to facilitate analysis and correlation.

4. **Correlation**
    - Analyze and correlate data to identify patterns and detect potential security threats that individual logs might not reveal.

5. **Alerting**
    - Generate alerts for identified threats and anomalies, often in real-time, to prompt immediate investigation and response.

6. **Dashboards and Reporting**
    - Provide intuitive dashboards and customizable reports to visualize security posture, trends, and compliance status.

7. **Forensic Analysis**
    - Enable detailed examination of security incidents to understand the root cause and impact, and to aid in remediation.

8. **Incident Management**
    - Track and manage security incidents through a formalized workflow, often integrating with ticketing and case management systems.

Benefits

1. **Enhanced Threat Detection**
    - Detect complex and advanced threats through correlation of data from multiple sources, identifying patterns that single-point solutions might miss.

2. **Improved Incident Response**

- Facilitate faster and more effective response to security incidents with real-time alerts and comprehensive forensic tools.

3. **Regulatory Compliance**
    - Help organizations meet regulatory and industry compliance requirements by providing detailed logs, audit trails, and compliance reports.

4. **Centralized Visibility**
    - Offer a centralized view of an organization's security posture, making it easier to monitor, manage, and protect the IT environment.

5. **Operational Efficiency**
    - Reduce the workload on security teams by automating the collection, analysis, and correlation of security data.

Challenges

1. **Complexity and Cost**
    - Implementing and managing SIEM solutions can be complex and expensive, requiring significant resources and expertise.

2. **False Positives**
    - SIEM systems can generate a high volume of alerts, including false positives, which can overwhelm security teams and obscure genuine threats.

3. **Scalability**
    - As organizations grow, the volume of log data increases, requiring SIEM solutions to scale accordingly to handle the data efficiently.

4. **Data Privacy**
   - Ensuring the privacy and security of the collected log data is crucial, especially when dealing with sensitive information.

Popular SIEM Solutions

1. **Splunk**
   - Known for its powerful search, monitoring, and analysis capabilities across various types of data.
2. **IBM QRadar**
   - Offers robust threat detection, incident response, and compliance management features.
3. **ArcSight**
   - Provides comprehensive security analytics and monitoring, favored for its scalability in large environments.
4. **LogRhythm**
   - Focuses on threat lifecycle management, providing end-to-end threat detection and response.
5. **Microsoft Sentinel**
   - A cloud-native SIEM solution that leverages Azure's capabilities for scalability and integration with other Microsoft security tools.

Conclusion SIEM solutions are essential components of modern cybersecurity strategies, providing organizations with the tools needed to detect, analyze, and respond to security threats effectively. By centralizing and correlating security data, SIEM solutions enhance visibility, improve incident response, and support compliance efforts. Despite challenges related to complexity and cost, the benefits of SIEM solutions make them invaluable for maintaining robust cybersecurity in an increasingly complex threat landscape.

Endpoint Detection and Response (EDR): A Comprehensive Summary

Introduction Endpoint Detection and Response (EDR) solutions are advanced security tools designed to monitor, detect, and respond to cyber threats on endpoints such as computers, mobile devices, and servers. EDR provides continuous and comprehensive visibility into what is happening on endpoints in real-time, enabling organizations to identify, investigate, and mitigate threats quickly and effectively.

Purpose The primary purpose of EDR solutions is to enhance an organization's ability to detect and respond to sophisticated threats that bypass traditional security measures. EDR focuses on identifying malicious activities and indicators of compromise (IOCs) on endpoints, providing detailed forensic analysis and enabling rapid response to mitigate potential damage.

Key Components EDR solutions typically include several critical components and functionalities:

1. **Continuous Monitoring**
    - Real-time monitoring of endpoint activities to detect suspicious behavior and anomalies.
2. **Threat Detection**
    - Identifying known and unknown threats using signature-based, behavior-based, and machine learning techniques.
3. **Incident Response**

- Providing tools and capabilities to respond to and mitigate detected threats, such as isolating affected endpoints, terminating malicious processes, and removing malware.

4. **Data Collection and Storage**
    - Collecting and storing endpoint data, including process information, file changes, registry modifications, and network activity, for analysis and forensic investigation.

5. **Analysis and Forensics**
    - Offering detailed analysis and forensic capabilities to understand the nature and scope of an attack, including root cause analysis and the attack timeline.

6. **Integration**
    - Integrating with other security tools such as Security Information and Event Management (SIEM) systems, Threat Intelligence Platforms (TIPs), and Network Traffic Analysis (NTA) tools to enhance overall security posture.

Benefits

1. **Enhanced Threat Detection**
    - Improved ability to detect sophisticated threats, including zero-day exploits, fileless malware, and advanced persistent threats (APTs).

2. **Rapid Incident Response**
    - Accelerated response to security incidents, minimizing the potential impact and reducing the time to remediation.

3. **Comprehensive Visibility**

- Greater visibility into endpoint activities and behaviors, providing insights into potential security incidents and vulnerabilities.

4. **Reduced Dwell Time**
    - Decreased time that threats remain undetected within an organization's network, thereby reducing potential damage.

5. **Improved Forensic Capabilities**
    - Enhanced ability to conduct detailed forensic investigations, understand attack vectors, and implement effective remediation measures.

Challenges

1. **Complexity and Resource Requirements**
    - Implementing and managing EDR solutions can be complex and require significant resources, including skilled personnel and infrastructure.

2. **Alert Fatigue**
    - High volume of alerts can lead to alert fatigue, where security teams may become overwhelmed and potentially miss critical incidents.

3. **Data Privacy**
    - Ensuring the privacy and security of collected endpoint data is crucial, especially when dealing with sensitive information.

4. **Integration**
    - Integrating EDR solutions with existing security tools and workflows can be challenging, requiring careful planning and coordination.

Popular EDR Solutions

1. **CrowdStrike Falcon**
    - Known for its cloud-native platform, real-time threat detection, and comprehensive response capabilities.
2. **Carbon Black (VMware Carbon Black Cloud)**
    - Offers advanced threat detection, incident response, and endpoint visibility features.
3. **Microsoft Defender for Endpoint**
    - Provides integrated threat detection and response capabilities, leveraging Microsoft's security ecosystem.
4. **SentinelOne**
    - Focuses on autonomous threat detection and response with machine learning and AI-driven capabilities.
5. **Sophos Intercept X**
    - Combines EDR with advanced endpoint protection, including anti-ransomware and exploit prevention.

Conclusion EDR solutions are essential components of modern cybersecurity strategies, providing organizations with the tools needed to detect, analyze, and respond to endpoint threats effectively. By offering continuous monitoring, detailed forensic analysis, and rapid incident response, EDR enhances an organization's ability to protect its endpoints from sophisticated cyber threats. Despite challenges related to complexity and resource requirements, the benefits of EDR solutions make them invaluable for maintaining robust endpoint security in an increasingly complex threat landscape.

Intrusion Detection Systems (IDS) / Intrusion Prevention Systems (IPS): A Comprehensive Summary

Introduction Intrusion Detection Systems (IDS) and Intrusion Prevention Systems (IPS) are critical components of an organization's cybersecurity infrastructure. Both are designed to monitor network and system activities for malicious activities or policy violations and respond accordingly. While IDS primarily focuses on detecting potential threats and alerting administrators, IPS can also take proactive measures to block or prevent those threats.

Purpose The primary purpose of IDS and IPS is to enhance the security of an organization's network by detecting, alerting, and responding to potential cyber threats. These systems help in identifying unauthorized access, policy violations, malware, and other types of cyber attacks.

Key Components and Functions

1. **IDS (Intrusion Detection System)**
    - **Monitoring and Detection**: Continuously monitors network traffic or system activities for signs of malicious behavior.
    - **Alerting**: Generates alerts to notify administrators of detected potential threats.
    - **Types of IDS**:
        - **Network-based IDS (NIDS)**: Monitors network traffic for suspicious activity.
        - **Host-based IDS (HIDS)**: Monitors individual host or device activities for anomalies.

2. **IPS (Intrusion Prevention System)**
    - **Monitoring and Detection**: Similar to IDS, IPS monitors network traffic and system activities.
    - **Prevention and Response**: In addition to detecting threats, IPS can take proactive measures such as blocking malicious traffic, dropping malicious packets, or reconfiguring firewall rules.
    - **Types of IPS**:
        - **Network-based IPS (NIPS)**: Monitors and protects the entire network.
        - **Host-based IPS (HIPS)**: Monitors and protects individual hosts or devices.

Benefits

1. **Enhanced Security**: Both IDS and IPS provide an additional layer of defense, helping to identify and mitigate potential threats before they can cause significant damage.
2. **Real-time Threat Detection**: Continuous monitoring enables the real-time detection of suspicious activities and potential attacks.
3. **Improved Incident Response**: By alerting administrators and taking preventive actions, these systems improve the speed and effectiveness of incident response.
4. **Compliance**: Helps organizations meet regulatory and compliance requirements by providing detailed logs and reports of security incidents.

Challenges

1. **False Positives and Negatives**: IDS and IPS can generate false positives (incorrectly identifying benign activity as malicious) and false negatives (failing to detect actual threats), which can overwhelm administrators and reduce effectiveness.
2. **Resource Intensive**: Implementing and managing IDS/IPS can be resource-intensive, requiring dedicated hardware, software, and skilled personnel.
3. **Encrypted Traffic**: The increasing use of encryption can make it challenging for IDS/IPS to inspect and analyze network traffic effectively.
4. **Evasion Techniques**: Advanced attackers may use evasion techniques to bypass detection by IDS/IPS.

Popular IDS/IPS Solutions

1. **Snort**
    - An open-source network IDS/IPS widely used for its robust detection capabilities and extensive rule sets.
2. **Suricata**
    - Another open-source IDS/IPS that offers multi-threading and high-performance detection capabilities.
3. **Cisco Firepower**
    - A comprehensive network security solution that includes advanced IDS/IPS features integrated with firewall capabilities.
4. **Palo Alto Networks Next-Generation Firewall**
    - Incorporates advanced IDS/IPS functionality with other security features like application control and threat intelligence.
5. **McAfee Network Security Platform**

- Provides comprehensive network protection with integrated IDS/IPS capabilities and advanced threat intelligence.

Conclusion IDS and IPS are essential tools for enhancing an organization's cybersecurity defenses. IDS focuses on detecting and alerting administrators to potential threats, while IPS takes a more proactive approach by preventing detected threats from causing harm. Despite challenges such as false positives and resource requirements, the benefits of real-time threat detection, improved incident response, and regulatory compliance make IDS/IPS crucial components of a robust security strategy. By continuously monitoring network traffic and system activities, these systems help organizations protect their critical assets and maintain a strong security posture in the face of evolving cyber threats.

Best Practices

Incident Response Planning

Incident Response Planning: A Comprehensive Summary

Introduction Incident Response Planning (IRP) is a critical component of an organization's cybersecurity strategy. It involves developing a structured approach for identifying, managing, and mitigating the effects of security incidents. Effective incident response (IR) helps organizations minimize damage, reduce recovery time and costs, and enhance their ability to handle future incidents.

Purpose The primary purpose of an Incident Response Plan (IRP) is to provide a clear, actionable roadmap for responding to cybersecurity incidents. This ensures that all relevant personnel know their roles and responsibilities during an incident, facilitating a coordinated and efficient response.

Key Components

1. **Preparation**
    - **Policy Development**: Establish policies and procedures for incident response.
    - **Team Formation**: Create an Incident Response Team (IRT) consisting of members from various departments such as IT, legal, communications, and HR.
    - **Tools and Resources**: Ensure the availability of necessary tools, technologies, and resources for detecting and responding to incidents.

- **Training and Awareness**: Conduct regular training and awareness programs for employees to recognize and report potential security incidents.

2. **Identification**
    - **Monitoring and Detection**: Use tools and processes to continuously monitor systems and networks for signs of potential incidents.
    - **Incident Reporting**: Establish clear guidelines for reporting suspected incidents, including who to notify and how to document initial findings.
    - **Classification and Prioritization**: Determine the nature and severity of the incident, and prioritize response efforts based on potential impact.

3. **Containment**
    - **Short-term Containment**: Implement immediate actions to prevent the incident from causing further damage, such as isolating affected systems.
    - **Long-term Containment**: Develop and implement strategies to maintain business continuity while addressing the root cause of the incident, such as applying patches or additional security controls.

4. **Eradication**
    - **Root Cause Analysis**: Identify the root cause of the incident to ensure it is fully understood and addressed.
    - **Removal of Threats**: Eliminate any remaining threats from the environment, such as removing malware or closing vulnerabilities.

5. **Recovery**
    - **System Restoration**: Restore affected systems and services to normal operation, ensuring they are free from compromise.
    - **Testing and Validation**: Verify that the affected systems are functioning correctly and securely.
    - **Monitoring for Recurrence**: Continue to monitor systems to ensure that the threat does not reappear.
6. **Lessons Learned**
    - **Post-Incident Review**: Conduct a thorough review of the incident, including what happened, how it was handled, and what can be improved.
    - **Documentation and Reporting**: Document all findings and actions taken during the incident, and prepare a comprehensive incident report.
    - **Continuous Improvement**: Use insights gained from the incident to update and improve the IRP, policies, and security controls.

Benefits

1. **Minimized Damage**: Effective incident response reduces the potential impact and damage of security incidents.
2. **Faster Recovery**: A well-prepared IRP enables quicker recovery and restoration of normal operations.
3. **Regulatory Compliance**: Helps organizations meet regulatory and legal requirements for incident response and reporting.
4. **Enhanced Security Posture**: Continuous improvement and learning from incidents strengthen overall cybersecurity defenses.

5. **Reputation Management**: Proper incident handling and communication help maintain stakeholder trust and protect the organization's reputation.

Challenges

1. **Resource Allocation**: Ensuring adequate resources (personnel, tools, time) for effective incident response can be challenging.
2. **Coordination**: Coordinating efforts across various departments and stakeholders during an incident requires clear communication and strong leadership.
3. **Evolving Threats**: Keeping up with constantly evolving cyber threats and adapting the IRP accordingly is a continuous challenge.
4. **False Positives/Negatives**: Distinguishing between legitimate threats and false alarms requires sophisticated detection and analysis capabilities.

Popular Incident Response Frameworks

1. **NIST Special Publication 800-61 Revision 2**
   - Provides guidelines for developing an effective incident response capability based on best practices.
2. **SANS Incident Handler's Handbook**
   - Offers practical guidance and a structured approach to incident response.
3. **ISO/IEC 27035**

- Provides a framework for incident management, including principles for planning, identification, assessment, and response.

Conclusion Incident Response Planning is a vital aspect of an organization's cybersecurity strategy, enabling swift and effective action to mitigate the impact of security incidents. By preparing in advance, identifying incidents promptly, containing threats, eradicating malicious elements, and recovering systems, organizations can minimize damage and ensure business continuity. Continuous learning and improvement from each incident further enhance the organization's ability to handle future threats, thereby strengthening its overall security posture.

Threat Intelligence

Threat Intelligence: A Comprehensive Summary

Introduction Threat intelligence (TI) is the process of gathering, analyzing, and applying information about potential and current threats to an organization's cybersecurity. This information helps organizations understand, predict, and mitigate various security threats, enabling proactive defense strategies.

Purpose The primary purpose of threat intelligence is to provide actionable insights into the tactics, techniques, and procedures (TTPs) of cyber adversaries. By understanding these threats, organizations can enhance their security measures, respond more effectively to incidents, and reduce the risk of cyber attacks.

Key Components

1. **Data Collection**
    - **Sources**: Gather information from various sources such as open-source intelligence (OSINT), dark web monitoring, internal logs, threat feeds, and intelligence-sharing communities.
    - **Types of Data**: Includes indicators of compromise (IOCs), IP addresses, domain names, malware hashes, and TTPs.
2. **Data Analysis**
    - **Correlation and Contextualization**: Analyze collected data to identify patterns and provide context, linking different pieces of information to understand the bigger picture.

- **Enrichment**: Augment raw data with additional information to increase its relevance and usability.

3. **Threat Intelligence Lifecycle**
    - **Planning and Direction**: Define the goals and scope of the threat intelligence program based on organizational needs.
    - **Collection**: Gather relevant data from various sources.
    - **Processing**: Convert collected data into a usable format.
    - **Analysis**: Interpret and analyze data to produce actionable intelligence.
    - **Dissemination**: Share intelligence with relevant stakeholders within the organization.
    - **Feedback**: Gather feedback to refine and improve the intelligence process.

4. **Types of Threat Intelligence**
    - **Strategic Intelligence**: High-level information about the threat landscape, providing insights into trends, motives, and long-term risks. Used by senior management for decision-making.
    - **Tactical Intelligence**: Information about TTPs used by threat actors. Helps in understanding how attacks are carried out and aids in planning defensive measures.
    - **Operational Intelligence**: Detailed information about specific attacks or campaigns. Used by security operations teams to enhance incident response.
    - **Technical Intelligence**: Data on specific indicators of compromise (IOCs) such as IP addresses, URLs, and malware signatures. Used by security analysts to detect and mitigate threats.

Benefits

1. **Proactive Defense**: Enables organizations to anticipate and mitigate threats before they can cause harm.
2. **Enhanced Incident Response**: Improves the speed and effectiveness of responding to security incidents.
3. **Informed Decision-Making**: Provides the necessary information for making strategic security decisions and prioritizing security investments.
4. **Threat Context**: Offers a deeper understanding of the threat landscape, helping to identify the most relevant threats to the organization.
5. **Collaboration**: Facilitates information sharing and collaboration with other organizations and threat intelligence communities.

Challenges

1. **Data Overload**: Managing and analyzing the vast amount of data collected from various sources can be overwhelming.
2. **Quality and Relevance**: Ensuring the accuracy, relevance, and timeliness of threat intelligence data is challenging.
3. **Integration**: Integrating threat intelligence into existing security operations and workflows can be complex.
4. **Skill Requirements**: Requires skilled analysts to interpret and apply threat intelligence effectively.

Popular Threat Intelligence Platforms and Tools

1. **ThreatConnect**

- A platform that provides threat intelligence aggregation, analysis, and sharing capabilities.

2. **Recorded Future**
    - Offers real-time threat intelligence insights using machine learning and natural language processing.

3. **FireEye Threat Intelligence**
    - Provides detailed intelligence reports and threat analysis based on global threat activity.

4. **IBM X-Force Exchange**
    - A threat intelligence sharing platform that allows collaboration and sharing of threat data.

5. **Anomali**
    - Provides threat intelligence solutions that help organizations detect, investigate, and respond to cyber threats.

Conclusion Threat intelligence is a critical component of modern cybersecurity strategies, enabling organizations to proactively defend against evolving cyber threats. By gathering and analyzing threat data, organizations can gain valuable insights into potential adversaries, enhance their incident response capabilities, and make informed security decisions. Despite challenges such as data overload and integration complexities, the benefits of a robust threat intelligence program make it an essential element of a comprehensive cybersecurity framework.

Employee Training and Awareness: A Comprehensive Summary

Introduction Employee training and awareness programs are essential components of an organization's cybersecurity strategy. These programs aim to educate employees about cybersecurity best practices, potential threats, and their roles in protecting the organization's information assets. By fostering a security-conscious culture, organizations can significantly reduce the risk of human error leading to security incidents.

Purpose The primary purpose of employee training and awareness programs is to equip employees with the knowledge and skills necessary to identify, prevent, and respond to cybersecurity threats. These programs help ensure that all employees understand the importance of cybersecurity and their role in maintaining a secure environment.

Key Components

1. **Regular Training Sessions**
   - **Onboarding Training**: Introduce new employees to the organization's cybersecurity policies, procedures, and expectations from the outset.
   - **Ongoing Training**: Provide continuous education through regular training sessions to keep employees updated on the latest threats and security practices.
   - **Role-Specific Training**: Tailor training programs to address the specific needs and risks associated with different roles within the organization.
2. **Awareness Campaigns**

- **Phishing Simulations**: Conduct simulated phishing attacks to test and improve employees' ability to recognize and respond to phishing attempts.
- **Security Newsletters**: Distribute regular newsletters or updates highlighting recent security incidents, new threats, and best practices.
- **Posters and Reminders**: Use visual aids and reminders placed in common areas to reinforce key security messages and behaviors.

3. **Policy and Procedure Education**
    - **Security Policies**: Ensure employees are familiar with the organization's cybersecurity policies, including acceptable use policies, password policies, and data handling procedures.
    - **Incident Reporting Procedures**: Educate employees on how to report security incidents or suspicious activities promptly and correctly.

4. **Interactive and Engaging Methods**
    - **E-Learning Modules**: Utilize online training modules that include quizzes, interactive scenarios, and videos to make learning engaging and effective.
    - **Workshops and Seminars**: Organize in-person or virtual workshops and seminars where employees can learn from experts and ask questions.
    - **Gamification**: Incorporate gamification elements, such as quizzes and competitions, to make training more enjoyable and motivating.

Benefits

1. **Reduced Risk of Human Error**
   - By educating employees, organizations can significantly reduce the likelihood of human errors that could lead to security breaches.
2. **Enhanced Security Posture**
   - Well-informed employees act as an additional line of defense, helping to identify and prevent potential threats before they can cause harm.
3. **Improved Incident Response**
   - Training ensures that employees know how to recognize and report security incidents quickly, enabling a faster and more effective response.
4. **Regulatory Compliance**
   - Many regulations and standards require organizations to provide regular cybersecurity training to employees. Meeting these requirements helps maintain compliance and avoid penalties.

Challenges

1. **Keeping Content Relevant**
   - Ensuring that training materials stay up-to-date with the latest threats and best practices can be challenging.
2. **Engagement and Retention**

- Keeping employees engaged and ensuring they retain the information provided in training sessions requires innovative and interactive approaches.

3. **Resource Allocation**
   - Allocating sufficient time and resources for comprehensive training programs can be difficult, especially for smaller organizations.

4. **Measuring Effectiveness**
   - Assessing the effectiveness of training programs and identifying areas for improvement can be complex.

Best Practices

1. **Regular Updates and Refreshers**
   - Regularly update training content to reflect the latest threat landscape and conduct refresher sessions to reinforce learning.

2. **Tailored Training**
   - Customize training programs to address the specific needs and risks associated with different roles and departments within the organization.

3. **Engagement and Interaction**
   - Use interactive and engaging training methods to keep employees interested and motivated to learn.

4. **Continuous Improvement**
   - Collect feedback from employees, monitor the effectiveness of training programs, and continuously improve the training content and delivery methods.

Conclusion Employee training and awareness programs are vital for building a robust cybersecurity culture within an organization. By educating employees on cybersecurity best practices, potential threats, and their roles in maintaining security, organizations can significantly enhance their overall security posture. Despite challenges such as keeping content relevant and engaging employees, the benefits of a well-implemented training program make it an essential element of a comprehensive cybersecurity strategy.

Emerging Trends

Artificial Intelligence in Cybersecurity

Introduction Artificial Intelligence (AI) is revolutionizing the field of cybersecurity by enhancing the ability to detect, analyze, and respond to cyber threats with unprecedented speed and accuracy. AI technologies, including machine learning (ML) and deep learning, are being integrated into various cybersecurity applications to improve threat detection, automate responses, and predict future attacks.

Purpose The primary purpose of using AI in cybersecurity is to bolster defenses against increasingly sophisticated cyber threats. AI helps in identifying patterns, anomalies, and potential threats in vast amounts of data, enabling organizations to respond proactively and efficiently.

Key Components

1. **Threat Detection and Analysis**
   - **Anomaly Detection**: AI systems can learn normal behavior patterns and detect deviations that may indicate a security threat.
   - **Behavioral Analysis**: AI analyzes user behavior to identify unusual activities that could signal insider threats or compromised accounts.
   - **Pattern Recognition**: Machine learning models can recognize patterns in data that are indicative of specific types of attacks, such as malware or phishing.
2. **Automated Response**

- **Incident Response Automation**: AI can automate routine response actions, such as isolating infected systems or blocking malicious IP addresses, to contain threats quickly.
- **Threat Hunting**: AI tools assist in proactive threat hunting by continuously scanning for indicators of compromise (IOCs) and other threat signatures.

3. **Predictive Analytics**
    - **Threat Prediction**: AI uses historical data to predict potential future attacks, allowing organizations to strengthen defenses in anticipation of specific threats.
    - **Risk Assessment**: AI models assess the risk level of various assets and activities, helping prioritize security efforts and resource allocation.

4. **Enhancing Security Operations Centers (SOCs)**
    - **Alert Prioritization**: AI helps reduce alert fatigue by filtering and prioritizing alerts based on their severity and relevance.
    - **Data Correlation**: AI correlates data from multiple sources to provide a comprehensive view of the security landscape and identify complex attack patterns.

Benefits

1. **Improved Threat Detection**
    - AI can detect sophisticated and previously unknown threats more effectively than traditional rule-based systems.
2. **Faster Response Times**
    - Automation and rapid analysis enable quicker detection and response, minimizing the impact of cyber incidents.

3. **Scalability**
   - AI systems can analyze vast amounts of data from diverse sources, making them suitable for large-scale cybersecurity operations.
4. **Reduced False Positives**
   - Advanced AI models can better differentiate between legitimate activities and malicious ones, reducing the number of false positive alerts.
5. **Resource Efficiency**
   - AI can automate repetitive tasks, allowing human analysts to focus on more complex and strategic activities.

Challenges

1. **Data Quality and Quantity**
   - AI systems require large amounts of high-quality data for training. Insufficient or poor-quality data can hinder the effectiveness of AI models.
2. **Adversarial Attacks**
   - Attackers may attempt to deceive AI systems through adversarial techniques, such as injecting false data or manipulating inputs.
3. **Complexity and Cost**
   - Implementing and maintaining AI-driven cybersecurity solutions can be complex and costly, requiring specialized skills and resources.
4. **Bias and Fairness**

- AI models can inherit biases from training data, leading to unfair or incorrect decisions. Ensuring fairness and accuracy is a significant challenge.

5. **Integration with Existing Systems**
    - Integrating AI solutions with legacy systems and existing cybersecurity infrastructure can be challenging and require careful planning.

Popular AI Applications in Cybersecurity

1. **Darktrace**
    - Uses AI to detect and respond to cyber threats in real-time by understanding the normal behavior of users, devices, and networks.

2. **Cylance**
    - Employs AI to predict and prevent threats before they execute, focusing on endpoint security.

3. **IBM QRadar Advisor with Watson**
    - Leverages AI to assist SOC analysts by correlating and analyzing security incidents and providing actionable insights.

4. **Vectra AI**
    - Uses AI to detect hidden attackers in real-time and automate threat hunting processes.

5. **CrowdStrike Falcon**
    - Integrates AI and machine learning to provide comprehensive endpoint protection and threat intelligence.

Conclusion Artificial Intelligence is transforming cybersecurity by enhancing the ability to detect, analyze, and respond to threats with greater speed and accuracy. By automating routine tasks, predicting future attacks, and providing deeper insights, AI empowers organizations to bolster their cybersecurity defenses and reduce the risk of cyber incidents. Despite challenges related to data quality, adversarial attacks, and integration, the benefits of AI in cybersecurity make it an essential tool for protecting against the evolving threat landscape.

Zero Trust Architecture: A Comprehensive Summary

Introduction Zero Trust Architecture (ZTA) is a security framework that operates on the principle of "never trust, always verify." Unlike traditional security models that rely on perimeter defenses, Zero Trust assumes that threats can exist both inside and outside the network. This approach requires strict verification for every user and device attempting to access resources, regardless of their location.

Purpose The primary purpose of Zero Trust Architecture is to enhance an organization's security posture by minimizing the risk of unauthorized access and data breaches. It achieves this by continuously validating every request as though it originates from an open network.

Key Components

1. **Identity Verification**
    - **Strong Authentication**: Implement multi-factor authentication (MFA) to ensure that users are who they claim to be.
    - **Identity and Access Management (IAM)**: Centralized control over user identities and access permissions, ensuring that only authorized users can access specific resources.
2. **Least Privilege Access**
    - **Role-Based Access Control (RBAC)**: Grant access based on user roles and the principle of least privilege, ensuring users have the minimum level of access necessary to perform their duties.

- **Just-In-Time (JIT) Access**: Provide temporary access to resources only when needed and revoke it when it is no longer required.

3. **Network Segmentation**
    - **Micro-Segmentation**: Divide the network into smaller, isolated segments to limit lateral movement of threats. Each segment enforces its own security policies and access controls.

4. **Continuous Monitoring and Assessment**
    - **Real-Time Monitoring**: Continuously monitor user and device activity to detect suspicious behavior and potential threats.
    - **Behavioral Analytics**: Use machine learning and analytics to identify anomalies in user behavior that may indicate a security breach.

5. **Endpoint Security**
    - **Device Posture Assessment**: Evaluate the security status of devices before granting access to ensure they meet predefined security criteria.
    - **Endpoint Detection and Response (EDR)**: Deploy tools that provide visibility into endpoint activities, detect threats, and enable rapid response.

6. **Data Protection**
    - **Encryption**: Ensure that data is encrypted both in transit and at rest to protect it from unauthorized access.
    - **Data Loss Prevention (DLP)**: Implement DLP solutions to monitor and control the movement of sensitive data across the network.

Benefits

1. **Enhanced Security**: By verifying every access request and limiting access based on strict policies, Zero Trust significantly reduces the risk of unauthorized access and data breaches.
2. **Reduced Attack Surface**: Micro-segmentation and least privilege access minimize the potential impact of a security breach by limiting the attack surface.
3. **Improved Compliance**: Zero Trust helps organizations meet regulatory requirements by enforcing strict access controls and continuous monitoring.
4. **Increased Visibility**: Continuous monitoring and real-time analytics provide better visibility into user activities and potential threats.

Challenges

1. **Complex Implementation**: Transitioning to a Zero Trust model can be complex and requires significant changes to existing infrastructure and processes.
2. **Resource Intensive**: Implementing and maintaining Zero Trust Architecture can be resource-intensive, requiring dedicated personnel and advanced technologies.
3. **User Experience**: Strict access controls and continuous verification can impact user experience and productivity if not managed carefully.
4. **Integration with Legacy Systems**: Integrating Zero Trust principles with legacy systems and applications can be challenging and may require additional solutions or modifications.

Popular Zero Trust Solutions

1. **Google BeyondCorp**
   - A security model that shifts access controls from the network perimeter to individual users and devices.
2. **Microsoft Azure AD Conditional Access**
   - Provides adaptive access policies based on user, location, device, and risk.
3. **Zscaler Zero Trust Exchange**
   - Offers secure access to applications and services based on Zero Trust principles, ensuring that every connection is authenticated and authorized.
4. **Palo Alto Networks Prisma Access**
   - Delivers Zero Trust network security by securing access to applications and data across hybrid and multi-cloud environments.
5. **Cisco Zero Trust**
   - A comprehensive approach that includes identity, device, network, and workload security to implement Zero Trust principles.

Conclusion Zero Trust Architecture represents a fundamental shift in cybersecurity, moving away from traditional perimeter-based defenses to a model where trust is never assumed and always verified. By implementing strict access controls, continuous monitoring, and micro-segmentation, Zero Trust significantly enhances an organization's ability to protect its data and resources from unauthorized access and cyber threats. Despite the challenges of complex implementation and resource requirements, the benefits of a robust and adaptive security posture make Zero Trust Architecture a crucial element in modern cybersecurity strategies.

Cyber Resilience

Introduction Cyber resilience refers to an organization's ability to continuously deliver intended outcomes despite adverse cyber events. It encompasses the ability to prepare for, respond to, and recover from cyber attacks while maintaining essential functions and minimizing harm. Cyber resilience goes beyond traditional cybersecurity measures by integrating risk management, business continuity, and organizational resilience.

Purpose The primary purpose of cyber resilience is to ensure that an organization can withstand and quickly recover from cyber incidents, minimizing disruption and damage to operations, reputation, and finances. It focuses on maintaining the integrity, availability, and confidentiality of information and systems in the face of both known and unknown threats.

Key Components

1. **Risk Management**
    - **Risk Assessment**: Identify and evaluate potential cyber risks to the organization's assets, operations, and stakeholders.
    - **Risk Mitigation**: Implement measures to reduce identified risks to an acceptable level.
2. **Preparedness**
    - **Incident Response Planning**: Develop and maintain an incident response plan that outlines procedures for detecting, responding to, and recovering from cyber incidents.

- **Training and Awareness**: Conduct regular training and awareness programs to ensure employees understand their roles and responsibilities in maintaining cyber resilience.

3. **Detection**
   - **Continuous Monitoring**: Implement tools and processes for real-time monitoring of networks, systems, and data to detect anomalies and potential threats.
   - **Threat Intelligence**: Utilize threat intelligence to stay informed about emerging threats and vulnerabilities.

4. **Response**
   - **Incident Response**: Execute the incident response plan to contain and mitigate the impact of cyber incidents promptly.
   - **Communication**: Ensure clear communication channels and protocols are in place to coordinate response efforts internally and externally.

5. **Recovery**
   - **Business Continuity Planning**: Develop and implement business continuity plans to ensure critical functions can continue or quickly resume after a cyber incident.
   - **Disaster Recovery**: Establish disaster recovery procedures to restore systems, data, and operations to their pre-incident state.

6. **Learning and Improvement**
   - **Post-Incident Analysis**: Conduct thorough reviews of cyber incidents to understand what happened, how it was handled, and what can be improved.

- **Continuous Improvement**: Update and enhance policies, procedures, and controls based on lessons learned from incidents and changes in the threat landscape.

Benefits

1. **Reduced Downtime**: Ensures quick recovery and minimal disruption to business operations during and after a cyber incident.
2. **Enhanced Security Posture**: Strengthens overall security measures and reduces vulnerabilities through proactive risk management and continuous improvement.
3. **Regulatory Compliance**: Helps organizations meet regulatory requirements and standards related to cybersecurity and data protection.
4. **Improved Stakeholder Confidence**: Builds trust with customers, partners, and stakeholders by demonstrating a commitment to robust cyber resilience practices.
5. **Adaptive Capabilities**: Enables organizations to adapt to evolving threats and changing environments effectively.

Challenges

1. **Resource Intensive**: Implementing and maintaining cyber resilience measures can be resource-intensive, requiring significant investment in technology, personnel, and training.
2. **Complexity**: Coordinating efforts across various departments and ensuring all aspects of cyber resilience are addressed can be complex.

3. **Evolving Threat Landscape**: Keeping up with the constantly changing threat landscape and adapting resilience strategies accordingly can be challenging.
4. **Integration**: Integrating cyber resilience with existing business processes, systems, and strategies requires careful planning and execution.

Best Practices

1. **Comprehensive Risk Management**: Continuously identify, assess, and mitigate risks through a structured risk management process.
2. **Regular Training and Drills**: Conduct regular training sessions and simulated cyber attack drills to ensure preparedness and effective response.
3. **Collaboration and Information Sharing**: Collaborate with industry peers, regulatory bodies, and cybersecurity organizations to share information and best practices.
4. **Robust Backup and Recovery**: Implement and regularly test backup and recovery procedures to ensure data and systems can be restored quickly.
5. **Adaptive Incident Response**: Develop a flexible incident response plan that can adapt to various types of cyber incidents and scales as needed.

Conclusion Cyber resilience is an essential aspect of modern cybersecurity strategy, focusing on the ability to withstand, respond to, and recover from cyber incidents. By integrating risk management, preparedness, detection, response, and recovery, organizations can ensure they are better equipped to handle cyber threats and minimize their impact. Despite challenges such as resource requirements and complexity, the benefits of a resilient organization—reduced downtime, enhanced security, regulatory compliance, and improved stakeholder confidence—make cyber resilience a critical goal for any organization.

Additional Reading and Resources

Books

- **"The Cuckoo's Egg" by Clifford Stoll**: A classic account of tracking a hacker.
- **"Countdown to Zero Day" by Kim Zetter**: Detailed account of the Stuxnet attack.

Online Courses

- **Coursera and edX**: Offer courses on cybersecurity fundamentals, advanced techniques, and specific topics like ethical hacking and incident response.

Websites and Blogs

- **Krebs on Security**: Brian Krebs' blog on security news and investigative journalism.
- **Dark Reading**: News and analysis on IT security.

Professional Organizations and Certifications

Organizations

- **ISACA (Information Systems Audit and Control Association)**
- **(ISC)² (International Information System Security Certification Consortium)**
- **SANS Institute**

Certifications

- **CISSP (Certified Information Systems Security Professional)**
- **CEH (Certified Ethical Hacker)**
- **CISM (Certified Information Security Manager)**

www.ingramcontent.com/pod-product-compliance
Lightning Source LLC
Chambersburg PA
CBHW082235220526
45479CB00005B/1236